Clean Your House & Everything in It

by Eugenia Chapman
& Jill C. Major

A PERIGEE BOOK

To obtain the best results with maximum safety,
the authors and the publisher recommend
that you read and follow the instructions provided in this
book and listed on the suggested cleaning aids
carefully and entirely *before* beginning any task.

A Perigee Book
published by
The Berkley Publishing Group
200 Madison Avenue, New York, NY 10016

First Perigee edition: March 1991
Copyright © 1991, 1982 by Eugenia Chapman and Jill C. Major
Published simultaneously in Canada

Library of Congress Cataloging-in-Publication Data
Chapman, Eugenia.
    Clean your house & everything in it by Eugenia Chapman &
Jill C. Major.
        p.   cm.
    Reprint. Originally published: New York : Grosset & Dunlap
Publishers, c1982.
    Includes index.
    1. Cleaning. I. Major, Jill C. II. Title. III. Title: Clean
your house and everything in it.
TX324.C48   1991   90-46280 CIP
648´.5—dc20
ISBN 0-399-51658-1

Cover design by Lisa Amoroso
Printed in the United States of America

20   19   18   17   16   15

This book is printed on acid-free paper.

CONTENTS

DEDICATION

To Barney B. Chapman, father and husband, for supporting and encouraging us. To Ken Major, husband and son-in-law, for cleaning the house while we were writing about it and for rekindling our enthusiasm when discouragement threatened the project. To Veda Jentzsch, grandmother and mother, for unselfishly passing down her housekeeping secrets. To Carol Gold, sister and daughter, for calling late one night and suggesting that we write a book (we laughed at the idea) and for spending many hours helping us organize the information. To Rachelle, Christopher, Melanie, Byron, Jason, Cameron, Pamela and Patricia, children and grandchildren, for without their cheerful patient sacrifices and helping hands, this book could never have been completed. And finally, to Brook, cousin and niece, and to Barney, David, Jeanne, Shirley, Sam, Jackie, Jim, Becky, Susan and their spouses, sisters and brothers, sons and daughters, for always being there to share our failures and successes and just because we love them.

Eugenia J. Chapman
Jill C. Major

Clean Your House & Everything in It

1 Cleaning Products & Tools

My Motto

Give me a warning,
I'll clean all morning.
No call first,
Expect the worst.
Either way,
You're welcome to stay!
    —Jill C. Major

The cleaning industry is a multibillion-dollar business, not only in the products sold, but also because of the furnishings that the cleaning products damage and destroy and that then have to be repaired or replaced. We laugh at advertisements that promise us sex appeal if we use a certain toothpaste. After all, everyone knows that it takes many factors, such as a good figure, a nice personality, and the right member of the opposite sex, to make a person attractive. But women seem to believe everything advertisements tell them about cleaning products, even though many that are sold on the market are too strong for the simple household dirt we fight everyday. It is like swatting a fly with karate or putting Muhammad Ali in the boxing ring with Mickey Rooney. It is just plain overkill, and someone or something is going to get hurt by it.

So we find in today's market hard-water cleaners that take the finish off of the shower tiles and the bathtub and make them look worse than they ever did with the hard-water spots; easy-to-use toilet bowl cleaners that you put in the tank and never have to worry about until they leave a permanent blue stain in the toilet bowl that is impossible to remove; spray furniture polishes that trap pollutants in the wood and damage it; wall cleaners that are too harsh; window cleaners that leave streaks; oven cleaners that are poisonous to smell or touch—the list goes on and on. And for all this you pay prices that you would refuse to pay for a sirloin steak.

Advertising may be described as the science
of arresting the human intelligence long enough to get money from it.
—Stephen Leacock

The cleaning methods in this book may be considered old-fashioned. When I give talks to women's groups, I often hear "I used to do that" among the older women. They stopped using the homemade methods because the market was flooded with "new" and "improved" products and soon they forgot all about these alternative ways to do things. This is ironic because as some of the new cleaners have gotten stronger the "old" dirt has gotten weaker. The beautiful new finishes on fabrics, floors, walls, and appliances are, in many cases, much easier to clean than their older counterparts.

Cleaning does not have to be harmful or expensive. Many everyday cleaners can be made by the gallon for under a dollar and they are easy to use. In fact, some of the best products sold in the stores are nothing more than old-fashioned mixtures that have been perfumed, colored, pre-mixed, and packed in a bottle or aerosol can with a pretty label added.

Advertising is 85 percent confusion and 15 percent commission.
—Fred Allen

CLEANING PRODUCTS

Always remember that every cleaning product is a potential hazard in your home. Keep all cleaning products away from children. A high, locked cupboard is the best safeguard. Never store cleaning products close to any heating element (above the stove or near the furnace). Many products are combustible. And never mix chlorine bleach with ammonia products, lye, toilet-bowl cleaners, rust removers, vinegar, oven cleaners, or any other cleaning agent. (Remember that cleansers contain chlorine bleach also.) Such combinations release a gas that, if inhaled, can cause injury or death.

With very few exceptions, I do not recommend the use of aerosols. They have long been suspected of contributing to health problems. People with heart conditions or lung problems should especially avoid them.

Only the young die good.
—Oliver Herford

If you cannot find a cleaning product you want or need, ask the store manager. He will usually be glad to order it for you!

BASIC CLEANING PRODUCTS

Most cleaners recommended in this book are already in your cleaning closet, like ammonia, cleanser, liquid bleach, dish soap, lemon oil, rubbing alcohol, and white vinegar. Some are found in the kitchen cupboard, such as baking soda, Coke, salt, tea, and cream of tartar, and some in your refrigerator, like yogurt and fresh lemons. Some tough problems require special cleaners that have to be bought in hardware or paint stores. Whenever I have recommended these products in this book, I have noted where they can be purchased.

BRAND-NAME CLEANERS

I have recommended the following products by brand name because I have tested them over the last thirty years in the beautiful, expensive homes that I work in, along with many other products, and have found them the best remedies for the cleaning problems described in this book. I am not paid in any way to promote or sell these products.

CLEANER	MANUFACTURER
Fels-Naptha (This is a brown bar of soap that is excellent for stain removal. It is usually found next to Lava hand soap in the grocery store.)	Purex Corp. Lakewood, CA 90712
Johnson's Jubilee Cleaner (liquid not spray)	S. C. Johnson & Son Racine, WI 53403
Howard's Feed 'N Wax	Howard Products, INC 411 W. Maple Ave. Monrovia, CA 91016
Lava (hand soap)	Procter & Gamble Cincinnati, OH 45202
Lysol Brand Disinfectant	Lehn & Fink Products Division of Sterling Drug, Inc. Montvale, NJ 07645
Lysol Toilet Bowl Cleaner	Lehn & Fink Products Division of Sterling Drug, Inc. Montvale, NJ 07645
Murphy's Oil Soap*	Murphy-Phoenix Company P.O. Box 22930 Cleveland, OH 44122

*This is a very important cleaner. Make sure your store stocks it. It can be purchased almost anywhere cleaning supplies are sold.

Naval Jelly	Duro Woodhill Permatex Loctite Corp. Subsidiary Cleveland, OH 44128
Old English Red Oil	Boyle-Midway Inc. 685 Third Avenue New York, NY 10017
Old English Scratch Cover for Light and Medium Wood for Dark Wood	Boyle-Midway Inc. 685 Third Avenue New York, NY 10017
Oven 'N Grill Spray Coating	Amway Corp Ada, MI 49355 *or*
Oven Spray (Keep It Clean)	Fuller Brush Great Bend, KS 67530
Pledge Lemon Oil	S.C. Johnson & Son, Inc. Racine, WI 53403
Rit Clothes Dye	Special Products Affiliate of CPC International, Inc. Indianapolis, IN 46221
Soilax	Economics Laboratories St. Paul, MN 55102
Spic and Span	Proctor & Gamble Cincinnati, OH 45202

CLEANING SOLVENTS

A cleaning solvent is a water-free chemical used in some cleaning recipes and a lot of stain-removal procedures. Thoro and Carbona are extremely flammable. Energine is nonflammable. All of them are dangerous if used improperly. Observe all the cautions recommended on the bottle.

12

Carbona	Carbona Products Co.
	Brooklyn, NY 11222
Energine	The d-Con Company, Inc.
	Subsidiary of Sterling Drug, Inc.
	Montvale, NJ 07645
Thoro	Thoro Products
	Box 504
	Arvada, CO 80001

WAXES

Bruce's Hardwood Floor Cleaner and Wax	Armour-Dial, Inc. Phoenix, AZ 85077
Glo-Coat	S. C. Johnson & Son
	Racine, WI 53403
Johnson's Paste Wax	S. C. Johnson & Son
	Racine, WI 53403
Tre-wax	Grow-Group
	Culver City, CA 90230
Tre-wax Hardwood Floor Cleaner	Grow-Group Culver City, CA 90230
Turtle Wax	Turtle Wax, Inc.
	Chicago, IL 60614

CLEANING TOOLS

BROOMS

A manmade fiber broom or a dust mop should be used for no-wax vinyl, wood, and marble floors. A straw broom is too harsh on these kinds of floors, but it is the best broom for all other surfaces. I also like a good straw broom for sweeping off the lint that collects on the edges and

13

corners of carpets. Buy a broom that has been cut on an angle for sweeping out corners.

Store a broom upside down or hung up above the floor. If it is stood on the straw or fibers it will lose its shape and its efficiency.

MOPS

I never use a mop to scrub floors. I prefer to be down where the dirt is. Mopping is very hard on floors if the floor is not wiped dry. Leaving the floor wet dulls and ruins the shiny surface.

The next best thing to hand-and-knee scrubbing is a spring mop. Your own heavy terrycloth rags can be attached to a spring mop for scrubbing and wiping. A big advantage in using a spring mop is that the rags can be removed for cleaning in the washing machine.

A self-wringing sponge mop is second best. After each use it should be rinsed, wrung out, and placed upside down in an open, airy place to dry.

I don't like string mops because they leave streaks. It is also hard to disassemble them for cleaning and drying, so eventually they start to smell bad and have to be replaced.

RAGS

As a hammer is to the carpenter, rags are to the housecleaner. I use old terrycloth towels on many cleaning problems, like scrubbing floors, walls, rugs, and upholstery. Kitchen towels do not absorb like bath towels and so they are not as good for cleaning. Old diapers are great, though.

Old percale or cotton sheets are very good for washing windows or other "soft" cleaning. Permanent-press materials are not good for rags. They are specially treated so that they do not absorb moisture. They skid over the water instead of drying it and cleaning whatever is underneath the cloth. Give the old permanent-press rags to your husband for painting and greasy car repairs.

Never add fabric softeners to the rags (or diapers). They leave a film that makes the rags less absorbent.

RUBBER GLOVES

I always use rubber gloves when I am cleaning. Water and mild cleaners dry out your hands, and harsher cleaners, like ammonia or turpentine, irritate the skin. Many cleaning jobs require hot water, which is uncomfortable on bare hands.

My favorite is Playtex Living Gloves. They are lined, which makes it easy to pull them on and off. The skin seems to perspire less in a lined glove than in an unlined one. (If you have problems with perspiring hands, sprinkle cornstarch or baby powder in the gloves. This will make them even easier to pull on and off.) The Playtex gloves last longer and they are easier to work in than any other brand that I have tried. Things won't slip out of your hands as easily, and small objects can be picked up when wearing them.

The second-best brand is Soft Touch. They are cheaper than Playtex, but they don't fit as well or last as long.

Playtex Living Gloves	International Playtex, Inc.
	Dover, DE 19901
Soft Touch	Eagle Hygienic Rubber Co.
	Division of Tops, EHR Corp.
	Brooklyn, NY 11237

Disposable gloves are good for some chores like polishing furniture with dark oil (this job will stain other rubber gloves), cleaning out a vacuum cleaner that doesn't have disposable bags, and painting. They cannot be used with hot water because they are not thick enough to protect the hands.

OTHER TOOLS

Dust Handler	Suburbanite P.O. Box 1000 Holliston, MA 01746
One-Wipe Dust Cloths	Guardsman Products, Inc. Grand Rapids, MI 49506
Pumice Scouring Stick	United States Pumice Company 20219 Bahama Street Chatsworth, CA 91311
Dr. Scholl's Smooth Touch Beauty Stone	Scholl, Inc. Memphis, TN 38151

STAINLESS-STEEL SCRUB PADS

These can be purchased in most grocery stores. Be cautious of those that are hard or stiff. They are harsh and can scratch the surfaces they are supposed to clean. The best quality of stainless-steel scrub pads feel soft and spongy. I recommend:

Brillo Stainless Metal Cleaning Pads	Dial Corp. Phoenix, AZ 85077
Chore Boy	Chore Boy Division Airwick Industries Inc. Carlstadt, NJ 07072
Mr. Scrubmaster Scrubber	Phoenixware 4022 S. 20th Street Phoenix, AZ 85040
Suburbanite Scouring Pads	Suburbanite P.O. Box 1000 Holliston, MA 01746

SOAP-FILLED PAD
SOS

Miles Laboratories, Inc.
Chicago, IL 60638

SCOURING PAD
Scotch Brite

Minnesota Mining & Mfg. Co.
3M Center
St. Paul, MN 55101

BRUSHES
Toilet Bowl Brush

Continental Bowl Brush
Empire Brush, Inc.
Greenville, NC 27835
(any brand)
Nylon scrub brush
Percolator brush
Refrigerator coil brush (purchase at
   appliance stores)
Toothbrush

PAPER TOWELS
Recommended for cleaning strength:
Bounty

Proctor & Gamble
Cincinnati, OH 45202

Brawny

American Consumer Products
Division of American Can
Greenwich, CT 05830

MISCELLANEOUS
Two gallon bucket
Vacuum cleaner (page 75)
Squeegee

17

YOUR NOTES & CLEANING RECIPES

_____

_____

_____

_____

_____

_____

_____

_____

_____

_____

_____

_____

_____

_____

_____

_____

_____

_____

2 Advice from a Pro (& Mother of Eleven)

Yes, I am the mother of eleven children and still "sane," though some days "institutionally unconfined" seems a better description. I am also a professional housekeeper with more than thirty years of experience, and I give lectures on the subject. I am often asked, "What is the toughest housecleaning problem?" I have tackled every kind of stain and dirt a family can produce, but these problems are minimal compared to the greatest housekeeping burden of all—guilt! Once you stop comparing yourself to an ideal, Polly Perfect housekeeper, you may find that you are quite satisfied with the order in your home. If so, then good for you. Go enjoy life! If you want to be a little better, then drop the guilt and get moving. Here's how to do it.

Each woman thinks the other woman's
house always looks the way it does on club night.

ORGANIZING YOUR HOUSECLEANING

Remember that keeping a house is not just one skill; it is a combination of many, many skills. Getting windows sparkling clean is a totally different skill from organizing cupboards efficiently. Maintaining shiny floors is a separate skill from retaining the satin finish on wood furniture.

First, make a list of all your housecleaning skills. (This doesn't help too much in becoming a better housekeeper, but it does cushion the shock of the next step a bit.)

Second, make a list of your weaknesses or skill deficiencies. Be honest, but not depressing. Give yourself credit for partial conquests.

Third, choose a realistic, easy goal from the second list. Studies show that any time you try to make a drastic change in your life the chance of failure is very high. Failing makes the project more miserable and discouraging on the next try, so make your goal as simple and as precise as possible. For example: "I'm going to vacuum the floor when it needs it instead of waiting until I know that company is coming." When you have worked this task into your routine, choose another goal.

Fourth, be patient with yourself. Becoming a better housekeeper takes knowledge and time. The basic knowledge is found in this book. It will teach you total care of everything in your house from the moment you buy it to that last fatal hour when children or pets destroy it.

Time, of course, is an individual matter, but most of us don't have enough of it. Learn to be a very clever impostor, by following a basic housekeeping rule that compensates for the lack of time: *Begin every cleaning effort by attacking those areas that visitors will see first.*

Housekeeping is like stringing beads
with no knot in the end.

THE QUICK ONCE-OVER

There are several things that stick out like a piece of black raisin caught in your front tooth:

1. **YOU.** Many women like to clean house in an old bathrobe, but getting caught that way at eleven in the morning can ruin the effect

of all your hard work. So get dressed and make yourself presentable before you start the cleaning. Then if a neighbor or salesperson stops by before you have things in order, you can at least close the door behind you and talk to them outside, and they won't be left with an impression of sloppiness.

Today a woman is supposed to think like a man,
dress like a queen, speak like a lady, and work like a dog.
—Anon.

Bonus tip: Even though a wife may want her husband to know she has been working hard all day, she shouldn't greet him at the door holding a broom and looking tired and bedraggled. Freshening up her hair, face, and clothes before he comes home is even more important if the house is not looking its greatest: he will care far less if he has an attractive mate to focus on.

2. **FRONT HALL AND LIVING ROOM.** These are the first areas that need to be attended to each day. Pay special attention to dirty windows, finger smudges on walls and doors, dust on furniture, and an unvacuumed carpet or dull and dirty floors. I have always been told that these things are the signature of a poor housekeeper, but sometimes they are also the trophy of a busy mother with small children to care for or a working mother who comes home tired at the end of the day. Still, they make a house look unclean and gloomy.

The FBI has more than ten million fingerprints.
So has every home with two or more kids in it.

3. **COBWEBS.**   I hate to walk into a house and see cobwebs. Like magic, they appear in the middle of nowhere just in time to sweep down and hit some finicky lady in the face. You can de-cobweb a three-story house in about twenty minutes. Put a damp towel or rag over a broom and brush away. If you have a rough or sparkled ceiling, then really wet the rag. It will knock a lot of sparkles down, but after they have been vacuumed up, you won't even miss them. For hard-to-reach places, put an old sock or pillow case over a yardstick or broom handle and secure it with an elastic band. If you try to do the job with your vacuum cleaner, it will probably never get done and if you do find time, it will take hours.

4. **CLUTTER.**   There are two types of clutter. The first is the kind that children make with their toys and paper cuttings and story books. Never worry about this kind of clutter. As the years go by it will cure itself all too soon. It even came to an end for me with my eleven children.

The second type is adult clutter. If you haven't used something within the last three years, get rid of it. Let it clutter up someone else's house. Take all the bun warmers, the extra broken toaster that you have been meaning to have fixed, the Tupperware that has been sitting around because you melted the lids in the dishwasher, out of the cupboard and store them somewhere else. Get rid of old newspapers and magazines. If you haven't found time to read them yet, you never will. Instead of building new closets or moving, try removing the outdated clothes from your closets. I recommended this prescription to a doctor I was working for, and one day he rumbled up my driveway with a station wagon full of old clothes. That year I made patchwork quilts and crayon aprons for all my children and grandchildren for Christmas.

Clutter: Things that are worth saving but haven't been put away, deposited on top of things that are not worth saving but haven't been thrown away, which have settled next to things you aren't sure what to do with.

—Jill C. Major

ONE ROOM AT A TIME

After all of these obvious problems are alleviated, it is time to start on the rest of the house. Turn on some good, loud rock music. (You may want to do this before you start on the front hall and living room.) Do not play something soft and dreamy—it will lull you into slow motion. Psychologists have proved that we work better, faster, and more efficiently if we have some music to really groove and move to.

Once you start your in-depth cleaning, tackle one room at a time. Trying to conquer the whole house at once is discouraging, because you can't see any progress for three or four hours. Once you pick up something, only put it down in the place where it belongs. (If we could only make this a family habit, it would eliminate half of the general cleaning problem.) If there is a basement or second floor, keep a box by the stairs and put in all the things that go down or up. When you make a trip, take everything with you at once.

There is a running controversy among housekeepers as to whether the furniture should be dusted first so that the dust can settle on the carpets and be vacuumed, or whether the carpets should be vacuumed first so that the dust can fly up around the furniture and be dusted. Dust on the furniture is more noticeable than dust on the carpets, so I recommend vacuuming first. Then, after you dust, at least the dust is out of eyesight.

WORKING WIVES AND MOTHERS

Women who work outside the home face a special dilemma: if no one is home all day, the house will be in the exact-same condition when you return to it as when you left it. With a little extra organization and determination, this can be turned into a great advantage.

Start in the evening. Before going to bed, have everyone in the family pick up after themselves while you take a quick look at the kitchen and remedy any extra little jobs that need to be done there.

Get up early enough so that you can spend ten minutes in the living room and hallway and five minutes in all the other rooms, restoring order, dusting and even vacuuming. When the time limit is over, then move on. You will be surprised at how much can be accomplished in such a short time, and it will stay that way all day long.

If the morning schedule is really tight, at least make sure that the dishes are off the kitchen table and your bed is made. Clearing the dishes before fixing dinner and making the bed before crawling into it are both irritating enough to make a grouch out of the most amiable person.

If all else fails, remember that doors were made to be shut.

A Tribute to Doors

The scum on my tub got no scrubbing today,
   But that's O.K.
The bathroom has a door.

I slept quite late and my bed is unmade.
   Company's coming, but I'm not afraid.
The bedroom has a door.

The cupboard shelves are bulging out.
   No time to clean! No good to pout.
The cupboard has a door.

The soap operas beat out the dishes again,
   But I can face it with a grin.
The kitchen has a door.

What do I do when the house is a mess,
   And the minutes are short? You probably guessed.
Go out and shut the door.

—Jill C. Major

SPRING AND FALL CLEANING

A time seems to come in every woman's life when she gets an uncontrollable urge to give her house a thorough cleaning. (Heaven help her, because no one else usually will!) Many women still follow the old-fashioned spring and fall schedule. Spring cleaning was unavoidable many years ago when coal stoves were used all winter, coating everything with a thick, greasy dirt. Fall cleaning had to be undertaken because the windows were open all summer, letting the dust sift and settle throughout the house. They both could have been abandoned when air conditioners and central heating were installed. This tradition is especially a burden to women who work outside the home. There just isn't enough time to tackle this gargantuan job, unless you use precious vacation days.

A modern alternative is to clean one room thoroughly at least once a month. It is easier to remember to do this if the same day is scheduled for cleaning. I try to reserve the first Saturday of each month for this purpose.

Rooms with a coal stove or fireplace should still be cleaned in the spring. The kitchen is the biggest job and it usually takes two days to do. It needs to be cleaned about every six months because cooking spreads greasy dirt on everything. Bathrooms may also need to be thoroughly cleaned every six months if there is a problem with mold and mildew.

I use an ancient method to determine what room to honor each month. I look around the house and decide which room is absolutely driving me crazy, then I start tearing it apart.

Women's minds are cleaner than men's—
they change them more often.
—Oliver Herford

Start with the closets and throw away or give away the clutter. Wash the shelves and then reorganize the remaining contents. If you are working in a bedroom, pull off the blankets, mattress pads, and pillows and run them through the dryer on the air-fluff cycle. Turn over the mattress. Regardless of where you are cleaning, move all the furniture to one side of the room, then work on the empty side. Vacuum the drapes and sheer curtains or put them in the dryer. Some types of sheers should be washed (see page 115). While the curtains are down, scrub the walls. Use the crevice tool on the vacuum cleaner to clean the edges of the carpet and the mopboards (baseboards), then vacuum or sweep the floor. I don't scrub the portions of carpets that have been under heavy furniture because they are protected from traffic and dirt. The only exception to this is a dirty ring on the carpet around the heat or air vent. If the room is uncarpeted, the floors should be washed. Hardwood and other waxable floors need to be waxed under the furniture at least twice a year or they may go brittle and small cracks will form on the surface.

When the floor is dry, move all the furniture to the clean side of the room and repeat the process.

After the furniture is back in order, vacuum the couches and chairs thoroughly. If the seat cushions and/or the back cushions are removable, vacuum the tops, bottoms, and sides and the area under the cushions. Use the crevice tool to vacuum around the upholstery buttons and tucks, and down in the crevices.

Give all the wood furniture a good cleaning (see page 96). Pull out the drawers and vacuum or dust the casing. These dark corners make luxurious nests for spider families.

Wash the chandeliers, light fixtures, and windows and, finally, scrub the middle of the floor.

Now, if it exhausts you just reading about all this hard work, then maybe you need to hire professional help; however, don't naively assume that all your heavy housecleaning woes will then come to an end.

Work doesn't scare me.
I can lie right down by it
and go to sleep.

HIRING A PROFESSIONAL HOUSEKEEPER

Many professional housekeepers now belong to unions. As with any union, there are rules and regulations that govern what a member may or may not do. For example, she may not be able to wash windows, because that job belongs to the window-washing union. She probably can't scrub the carpet, because that would intrude on the carpet-cleaning union. She might not be allowed to move any heavy furniture or climb a ladder, because her insurance may not cover her if she does. Some jobs, like cleaning out a closet or washing walls, might require separate bids. If so, they will be an extra, added-on expense to the housekeeper's hourly wage. In fact, some professional housekeepers only sweep, vacuum, and dust, so check with the local union or ask the housekeeper what she will and will not do before you hire her.

When hiring a professional housekeeper, always require references. And when you call her past or current employers, ask very specific questions: (1) Is she honest? A cleaning person has freer access to your home than your very best friend. You need someone who will dust off, not rip off, your valuables. (2) Does she gossip about her clientele? The person who cleans out your closets and makes the beds gathers a lot of private information. It is not hard to tell if you are not sleeping with your husband, what the undyed color of your hair is, or if you read dirty books

27

or magazines on the sly. (If you don't care what the neighbors know, then you don't need to worry about this question.) (3) Is she a good worker? A slow worker or one who takes a lot of breaks is very expensive in terms of wages paid per work done. If you are going to hire someone you know is slow, then ask for a bid on the job. You will probably come out ahead.

Really good professional housekeepers are hard to find and harder to keep. Most will have a waiting list for their services and they can pick and choose their clientele. If you want a housekeeper to come back, always remember that she is a professional, not just the lowly "cleaning lady." She works hard, so feed her a good lunch (peanut butter or tunafish sandwiches are strictly for kids), and talk to her as an equal. If you follow this counsel you will not only keep your professional housekeeper, but you will probably make a lifelong friend. Many of my friends are clients, and all of my clients are friends.

PUTTING HOUSEWORK IN ITS PLACE

Don't make a clean house more important than you. A housewife should take time for herself every day and do something that the kids, the dog, and the husband cannot undo. Read a good book, take a walk, enjoy a hobby—and don't feel guilty about it. A short period of mental or physical recreation is as refreshing as a vacation (sometimes it is even more refreshing because you don't have to spend a week in a small car with screaming kids). Do not save your life for that day in the distant future when you will have the time. The savings that are deposited in a time bank are not insured against sickness, disaster, or death.

The time that you enjoy wasting is not wasted time.
—Laurence J. Peter

And finally, never let a structure of wood and brick take priority over people. Enjoy a good laugh when your toddler escapes from the bathtub and runs through the house naked, even if he is dripping water on your newly waxed floor. Don't be afraid of messing up the kitchen to prepare your husband's favorite foods or bake cookies for the kids. Greet your unexpected company with open arms and big smiles and forget about the dirty underwear festooning the bathroom. Wring every moment out of these times and hundreds more like them. Long after the fun and laughter have died down and the dinner table is quiet (a blessing every mother hopes for, but doesn't enjoy all that much when it is a permanent guest), the housework will still be there—always beckoning, calling, demanding.

———

Never hurry and don't worry.
You're here for just a short visit, so don't forget
to stop and smell the flowers.

———

YOUR NOTES & CLEANING RECIPES

_____

_____

_____

_____

_____

_____

_____

_____

_____

_____

_____

_____

_____

_____

_____

_____

_____

_____

3 The Uncleaners

Insanity is hereditary.
You can get it from your children.
—Sam Levenson

Many women find the effort spent in trying to motivate a family to do their part of the household chores is often more energy-draining and tiring than doing them ourselves. It is a major cleaning problem in most women's lives, and the only way it can be handled is with psychological muscle.

At times I used to look at my family and wonder if under those beautiful, impish smiles there really didn't beat hearts of pure gears, cogs, and springs. When I asked them to clean their rooms or pick up their clothes, I seemed to hear a definite whine and squeak that would finally grind out the feedback, "It does not compute!"

Oh, how I wished then that there really was a little man who rowed around in the toilet tank. I would have instructed him to scream at the little ones as they were leaving the bathroom, "Don't forget to flush!" That giant-sized, bald-headed jinni in the liquid-cleaner commercials could have come in handy to pop in every morning and intimidate the teenagers into making their beds. But most of all, think of having a sparkling knight on a white charger always trotting down the street to remind your husband that if you stumble over those cast-iron work boots in the front room one more time, there is an alternative. (Of course, it would be worse to run off with the knight. Can you imagine polishing that gold-plated armor every day, scrubbing down a mangy horse, and bleaching his mud-splattered doublet and hose? The grass isn't always greener on the other side, especially if horse droppings are doing the fertilizing.)

CHILDREN

Cleaning your house while your kids
are still growing, is like shoveling the walk before it stops snowing.
—Phyllis Diller

Like so many other mothers, I peeked in at my children at nap time and thought how peaceful and angelic they looked while they slept. I had to run over to the neighbor's to return a borrowed item, so I quietly slipped out of the house for a few moments. When I returned there was a dense white fog steaming out the front screen door. I ran in a panic. As I opened the door I could barely make out three little Pillsbury dough men with a twenty-five-pound bag of flour torn open in the middle of the front-room floor. The baby's diaper and shirt were filled with little handfuls of the white stuff.

"What are you doing?" I gasped and choked.

"We're powdering the baby, Mama!" they squealed with delight.

After I screamed, which sent the little culprits scurrying out of reach, I sat right down and cried. It took days to get the white film off the curtains, furniture, bedding, and rugs. Now that I look back on it, I wish that I had allowed myself a little chuckle. Cursing or laughing, I still had to clean it up.

I have not found any way to prevent children from having those "creative accidents," but I have learned two things that made me feel better about them. First, almost every cleaning disaster is humorous after a little time passes. Second, I can at times find sweet revenge in recounting to my grandchildren the things their parents used to do.

Before I got married I had six theories
about bringing up children;
now I have six children and no theories.
—Lord Rochester (1647–1680)

The messes that our children make are not the only challenge for a parent. I hope it is an obvious fact that children need to learn how to work when they are very young. It not only takes some of the burden from the household chores, but it makes children feel needed and important. If a child is having trouble in school, one of the first things a wise teacher or psychologist will ask is, "Do you give him/her responsibilities at home?"

The persons hardest to convince they're
at the retirement age are children at bedtime.
—Shannon Fife

David O. McKay once said, "Let us realize that the privilege to work is a gift, that power to work is a blessing, that love of work is success." Children need this gift to be successful and happy. Parents can help them obtain it by whistling, singing, and smiling when they are doing their own work; inventing little games and rewards for their children on work day; and giving each child a job that he or she can accomplish with pride.

Some parents keep a job chart. One of my daughters has a job dart board. The children throw the darts and whatever chore it hits is theirs for the day. Another of my daughters has a candy store in her bedroom. Each chore is worth a certain number of points. When her children have finished their work, they can use their points to go shopping in the candy store.

Rewards and games are fun, but remember that work has its own built-in prizes as well. Straightening Mama's and Daddy's shoes teaches a child to find pairs. Helping sort out the dirty laundry is a good time to learn colors. While setting the table, a child learns to count. Folding diapers and towels helps exercise fine hand coordination, and vacuuming and sweeping builds up large motor coordination. Children take pride in these skills as well as in their work.

By the time the youngest children
have learned to keep the place tidy, the oldest grandchildren
are on hand to tear it to pieces again.
—*Christopher Morley*

There are always favorite chores and chores that children consider nasty. Most children love to dust or to spray windows and mirrors and wipe fingerprints away. These tasks hold a kind of magic for children of the "now you see it, now you don't" variety. Cleaning the bedroom, however, seems to be the most tedious and hated job for any child. Clothes never land in the hamper if it has a lid. Try using a new tall, round garbage pail for dirty clothes. Make a game of throwing the clothes like a basketball or football into the target. If you or your husband are handy, you could even install a hoop above the hamper. Both boys and girls really go for this.

Bachelors' wives and old maids' children are always perfect.
—S. R. N. Chamfort

Beds should be as simple as possible to make. The fancy, frilly coverlet is really not all that necessary at first. In the summer, a single sheet that has to be pulled over the pillow is quite sufficient. In winter, an added quilt isn't too difficult even for a preschooler to manage. At first, it may not look as good as you would like it to, but remember that a child is proud of any little accomplishment. Don't shatter their world by doing it over for them or by being critical of their efforts.

With luck, you can get your children motivated by work charts, games, and humor. When these things do not move them, however, I still believe that at times a child has to be raised "from the bottom up."

To bring a child up in the way he should go,
travel that way yourself once in a while.
—Josh Billings

TEENAGERS

People who wonder where this younger generation is heading would do well to consider where it came from.

To survive the teenage years, a mother must acquire some superhuman powers. She needs to be faster than a speeding bullet when cleaning and vacuuming the front room before someone's date shows up; more powerful than a locomotive to wrestle the toddler out of his sister's room after he has discovered the joys of makeup and perfume; and able to leap to the store in a single bound to get pantyhose, Certs, Kotex, and other emergency supplies. X-ray vision also comes in handy, to find lost shoes, lunch money, and school books.

---

*When I was a boy of fourteen my father was
so ignorant I could hardly stand to have the old man around.
But when I got to be twenty-one I was astonished
how much the old man had learned in those seven years.*
—Mark Twain

I have decided, after raising eleven teenagers, that as far as housekeeping goes, you can train children in the way they should go and when they become teenagers they will do their own thing regardless. Take my two oldest sons, who are only fifteen months apart. Barney has black hair and a dark complexion; David is blond and fair. In school they were in the same class once and the teacher never even suspected that they were brothers. In housekeeping, Barney was night and David was day. Barney "hung" his garments in the corners of the room, on the dresser, and under the bed. David was so meticulous that he had to iron his own clothes. He would spend half an hour making sure that one crease in a pant leg was perfect.

---

*Keep your teenagers at home.
Love them, communicate with them,
and hide the car keys!*

I trained all my children alike, but even now I wonder, where did I go wrong, or on the other hand, where did I go right? I screamed, lectured, sicked their Dad after them, and on occasion, I swatted them with the broom.

In weighing your own sanity against keeping peace in the home, maybe the best solution is to just close the door and nail a sign to the outside which reads, "Condemned by the Board of Health. Enter at your own risk!"

Sometimes college bred is just a four-year loaf.

The only thing wrong with the younger generation is that most of us don't belong to it anymore.

There is one bright side to this teenage cleaning dilemma. Surprisingly, some of the worst teenage mess-makers end up becoming the cleanest adult housekeepers. My son Barney is now a successful businessman. He is as well organized and as meticulous at home and in his personal dress as his brother David. It is the same story with all my children that gave me problems. This caterpillar-butterfly transformation was really puzzling until my daughter explained it to me. She said, "It didn't matter if we made a mess at home, because that was your house and we knew that you would clean it up. Now, if we don't pick up after ourselves, we know that no one else will and we want our homes to be as clean and as comfortable as the one we grew up in."

Who would have thought that such a pain in the neck could become such a lump in my throat!

HUSBANDS

A good marriage is between
a blind wife and a deaf husband.
—*Michel de Montaigne (1533–1592)*

Harlan Miller once said, "Often the difference between a successful marriage and a mediocre one consists of leaving about three or four things a day unsaid." I agree, but it is so hard to do when a husband has never learned that there are two sides to a hamper, the inside and the outside.

Women with messy husbands nag, plead, pout, and have tantrums, but usually to no avail. I believe that there are two ways to handle an uncooperative husband. The first way should be used with a man with a conscience, who is fairly neat in his personal mannerisms and wants his surroundings to be the same. The strategy is simple: if he drops his underwear on the bathroom floor, just leave it. If he hangs a dirty shirt on the bedroom doorknob or throws his socks and pants in the corner, let them stay. Just make sure that you keep the rest of the house spotless. When he begins to complain about the mess, tell him in a sweet and soft but very tired voice, "I'll pick up my things if you'll pick up yours." This should get the message across.

People who throw kisses are hopelessly lazy.
—*Bob Hope*

     If it doesn't, your husband is probably of the slob variety and you will have to resort to more dramatic methods. For example, wait until your husband is really relaxed in his favorite chair, reading his favorite sports magazine. From the bathroom or bedroom, scream as loud as you can while jumping up and down and waving your arms. Your husband will surely rush right in. When you have his attention, open the hamper lid several times and let it drop very slowly. Smile sweetly and say, "Guess what I discovered, dear? The hamper has a lid!"

Many married couples have learned that a
joke can be the shortest distance between two points of view.
—J. P. McEvoy

If none of these tactics works and your husband can't seem to give up his sloppy ways, don't be tempted to trade him in for a new model. After all, as Barbra Streisand asked, "Why does a woman work ten years to change a man's habits and then complain that he's not the man she married?" When all else fails, you might as well love him the way he is. A time may come when you would be grateful to trip over his shoes or pick up his suit coat one more time.

YOUR NOTES & CLEANING RECIPES

_____

_____

_____

_____

_____

_____

_____

_____

_____

_____

_____

_____

_____

_____

_____

_____

4 Bathrooms

Ode to Bathrooms

Smelly bathroom off my hall,
Toothpaste splattered on the wall,
Germs in toilet, growing wildly,
Scum and mold that sprout more mildly,
Underpants, a sweaty shoe,
Family glass that froths with flu;
Our ancestors no sense did lack—
They kept the "john" way out back!
                              —Jill C. Major

BATHTUB AND SINK

For an occasional scrub, cleanser is still the best cleaner. I have used it for years in my own tub and sinks and in the tubs and sinks of people I work for. I've never had problems with it scratching or dulling the porcelain. Many women make the mistake of leaving the tub or sink wet after rinsing. Wiping it dry with terrycloth rags (old bath towels) protects the finish.

DARK STAINS

If dark coloring is bleeding through the porcelain in the tub or sink, it may mean that the finish has been worn off. This may happen with many

41

years of wear, but usually it is caused by repeated use of harsh chemical cleaners. (If a cleaner gags or chokes you when you are using it, it probably contains a high concentration of acid or lye. I seldom use these types of cleaners.) If the finish has been worn away, then it has to be refinished by a professional or replaced.

If the finish hasn't been removed, then there are several methods that can be used to get rid of dark stains. The easiest is to dip a damp rag in baking soda and scrub. If that doesn't work, pour lighter fluid (used in cigarette lighters) *or* hydrogen peroxide on a rag and scrub the stain.

RUST

Light rust can be removed with a fresh lemon cut in half and dipped in salt. Rub it in and rinse it out. For worse problems, buy Naval Jelly (page 12). This can be purchased in hardware stores or drugstores. It is a really good cleaner and will take out many different types of stains. Don't get it on the faucets or other fixtures, though, because it may turn them dark or pit them.

YELLOW STAINS

Sometimes the whiteness of a tub or sink can be temporarily restored. Mix ½ cup of turpentine and 2 tablespoons of salt in an old dish or can. Dip a terry cloth rag in the mixture and scrub. Then, to give the tub or sink a pretty luster, polish it with liquid Johnson's Jubilee Cleaner. Don't put it on the tub floor, though, because the wax will make it slippery and the next person to use it might have an accident.

I believe in getting into hot water. It keeps you clean.
—*K. G. Chesterton*

SHOWERS

If water can carve out the Grand Canyon or soak out the worst burned-out crud in your pots and pans, then think about what it will do when left dripping on the shower walls and floor. This is what causes hard-water stains and mold. The worst part of your shower headache would be alleviated if you could just teach your family to wipe down the shower or tub after they were finished bathing. It doesn't take an extra rag. They have a giant-sized bath towel that they are going to throw in the dirty clothes anyway.

If you can't get them to do it that way, then buy a squeegee. Put it in the bathroom and let them squeegee down the shower after each use. They'll have a ball doing it while they are naked. Be sure to get a squeegee with a red rubber blade. Sometimes a black blade leaves marks.

People and clothes have a lot in common.
Both are wash-and-wear, but only the new ones stay wrinkle-free.
—Jill C. Major

FORMICA, TILE, AND CERAMIC

If the shower is only mildly dirty, then lemon oil will clean it beautifully. Pour a generous amount of the oil on a soft rag and wipe the shower walls. It will take several applications to cover the whole shower. With a clean cloth, rub the shower dry. Some people like to put lemon oil in a spray bottle and spray it on the shower. This works well too, but be sure to cover the floor of the shower or bathtub with a towel or other rag, because the oil will make it slippery.

43

If the shower is really moldy or has bad hard-water stains, use Lysol Toilet Bowl Cleaner. It will not harm the shower. This is strong medicine, but not nearly as strong as some of the hard-water cleaners on the market that really gag you. Squirt the Lysol Cleaner on the shower walls and scrub with an SOS pad or a nylon brush. Don't get the cleaner on the metal fixtures. It will pit them and turn them dark. Be sure to use rubber gloves to protect your hands. Rinse the shower and wipe it dry.

A sign to be hung on the door
for a mother with lots of children:
BATHROOM—Seating Capacity One!

FIBERGLASS, MARBLE, SIMULATED MARBLE

These types of showers are difficult to keep clean. They require a lot of extra work or they look terrible all the time. It is very important to make sure that marble and fiberglass showers are wiped dry after each use. Dullness, staining, and pitting are caused by water that has been allowed to drip down the shower walls and air-dry.

Go to the dealer that sold you the shower and buy their cleaner. This will do the best job of cleaning and it will remove many of the stains. The cleaner is strong, so use rubber gloves and open all the windows while using it.

The pitting is permanent, but it can be partially covered by rubbing the shower with Turtle Wax (white-paste car wax) or by using the wax sold by the dealer. Let the wax dry for about twenty minutes, then buff it with a terrycloth rag. The wax is a good protection against future staining. It should be applied about once a week.

SHOWER FLOORS

Wet the floor and sprinkle with powdered dishwater soap. Scrub with a nylon brush or soap-filled pad. If this doesn't work then make a paste out of 1/2 cup turpentine and 2 tablespoons salt. Using rubber gloves, rub it on the floor, scrub with SOS or nylon brush, rinse, and wipe dry.

GROUT

Mold, mildew, and stains seep right into *plastic* grout and they are almost impossible to get out. The grout has to be scraped off and replaced. If company is coming and you want to hide the black marks, apply white shoe polish with a double-tipped swab, like Q-tip. It stays on for a long time and it is a good cover-up.

Cement grout is beautiful and easy to keep up. Most hard water and mold can be taken out with lemon oil. If that doesn't work, dip a stainless-steel sponge (page 16) in denture cream toothpaste (the type used to clean false teeth) and scrub. This method is great for cleaning hard to reach corners.

SHOWER DOORS

Lemon oil will remove most stains, except deep-rooted stains like perfume. Put lemon oil on a rag, scrub the door, and wipe it dry with a clean rag.

If the stains are too stubborn for the lemon oil to handle, then squirt Lysol Toilet Bowl Cleaner on the door. Scrub, rinse, and wipe dry.

To clean the track, add 1/4 cup Spic and Span, Soilax or Ammonia to 1 quart of hot water. Use an SOS pad or stainless-steel pad to scrub. Corners can be reached by using a knife or a screwdriver with a rag wound tightly around it and dipped in the cleaning solution. To make the track easier to clean next time and keep the scum from sticking to the metal, apply some household oil.

It is impossible to enjoy idling
thoroughly unless one has plenty of work to do.
—Jerome K. Jerome

SHOWER CURTAINS

Do the shower curtains on the day you have a load of towels to wash. Load the wash lighter than normally and throw in the shower curtain. The friction of the bath towels around the curtain takes out the hard-water stains and cleans it. Don't let the curtain go through the spin cycle. Hang it outside or over the empty curtain rod in the bathroom and let it drip dry. When it's dry, put the curtain in the dryer on a heat cycle for about five minutes. This will take the wrinkles out.

If the shower curtain is badly stained, then take it outside and spray it well with a prewash spray (such as Spray & Wash or the prewash spray formula on page 139), before washing it with the towels.

MILDEW

To discourage mildew growth on tile and showers, dip a rag in turpentine and rub it in the mildew areas. Do this every three months or whenever mildew starts to show.

PAINT AND CEMENT

Drippings of paint or plaster in the shower or bathtub are a common problem for people who move into new homes. If the paint hasn't hardened, it can be removed with a wash-away paint remover. If the paint or cement has dried, make a thick paste out of trisodium phosphate (found in paint and hardware stores) and water. Spread this over the cement or paint drippings and let it stand for one hour. Scrub with a nylon brush or SOS pad. Cleanser will take off any black SOS marks. SOS is second choice because sometimes steel wool will make the finish go dull. If this happens, restore the finish by making a thick paste of powdered chalk (found in hardware stores) and water. Rub this on the shower and wipe it dry with a rag. To give the shower a shine, rub the walls with a lemon oil. A razor blade can also be used to remove hardened paint, but be careful. It may scratch the surface of the bathtub or shower.

I want a house that has got over all its troubles;
I don't want to spend the rest of my life
bringing up a young and inexperienced house.
—Jerome K. Jerome

FIXTURES

If the fixtures are in good shape and there isn't any hard-water buildup, then cleaning them with rubbing alcohol or lemon oil will really make them shine. Pour it on a rag, scrub the fixtures, and wipe dry.

If there is a lot of hard-water buildup, apply a thick coating of lemon oil and let it soak on the tap for at least an hour. This will soften the hard-water stain. Use a stainless-steel pad and scrub. Don't worry about marring the tap. I've used stainless-steel pads on gold and brass fixtures, and the ones put out by Amway or Fuller Brush do not scratch. Wipe the fixture dry.

Another way to get rid of hard-water stains is to sprinkle baking soda over the fixture and then pour white vinegar on it. Wrap a terry rag around the fixture and let it soak for at least an hour. Scrub with a stainless-steel pad.

To get in the really tight corners behind the faucet where the scum **47** collects and grows, use a toothbrush. Be sure to mark it "cleaning" or "scum brush" to deter the rest of the family from picking it up accidently. Put it with the cleaning supplies—it's a handy cleaning tool.

BATHROOM
Nature's call answered here!

TOILETS

There are some very harsh toilet-bowl cleaners on the market. Most of them are more powerful than the average housewife needs if she is cleaning her toilets weekly. One janitor was using a very strong commercial toilet-bowl cleaner in the employees' bathrooms. After he brushed out the toilet, he would use the cleaner to wipe off and disinfect the lids. The poor women employees would come out of the bathroom with big holes in their pantyhose. The cleaner had disintegrated them!

I use Lysol Toilet Bowl Cleaner for heavy jobs. It is mild, yet it cleans. For weekly cleaning, Efferdent or Polident Denture Tablets are wonderful. Just drop two in the bowl, let them dissolve, brush, and flush. If I don't have them on hand, I use cleanser, ammonia, or dish soap. On most toilets they do an effective job.

I prefer a Continental Bowl Brush (page 17). It does a better job than any other toilet brush I have tried. It doesn't have a wire in it, so it won't scratch the surface, and it lasts for years. Most leading grocery stores carry it in the cleaning section.

RINGS

If you have been using a strong toilet-bowl cleaner and have let it soak and bubble for a while each time you poured it in, you may notice a ring around the toilet that is impossible to scrub out. What has usually happened is that the cleaner has corroded the toilet finish at the water level. Without the protection of the finish, the stains soak in and make a dark ring. It is easy to tell if this is what is causing the problem by just feeling the inside of the bowl. The texture will be rougher around the ring than on the rest of the bowl. The only thing that can be done when this happens is replace the toilet. If you like a strong toilet-bowl cleaner, then be sure to brush immediately and flush several times to get it out of the bowl and plumbing. Also beware of toilet cleaners that are dark blue. They can leave a stain that is permanent. When using them, brush immediately and flush.

For other types of rings, pour a bucket of water down the toilet bowl or plunge it with a toilet-bowl plunger. This forces the water level below the ring and makes it accessible to work on. If the ring isn't too bad, pour a can of Coke around the stain. Let it soak for a few minutes and brush.

If the stain is really stubborn, buy a pumice stone or beauty stone. They are usually sold with the Dr. Scholl's foot care products in your local grocery store. Or, in the cleaning department, buy a Pumice Scouring Stick (page 16). Pour a bucket of water down the toilet bowl to force the water level below the ring, then scrub. These products will remove the ring and will not scratch the surface.

URINE SMELLS

Many housewives complain that the other sex gets distracted using the toilet and this tends to leave a bad smell on the floor around the toilet-bowl cleaner. When scrubbing the bathroom floor, add 1 tablespoon of Lysol to the wash water. Pour a little undiluted Lysol around the base of the toilet or put Lysol in a spray bottle and squirt it between the floor covering and the toilet. This has a strong smell of its own, but it is much to be desired over the odor of urine. Once you get rid of the smell, buy a tube of adhesive caulking and seal the crack between the toilet and the floor so that moisture won't get under there again. With a little practice, caulking is easy to apply, and it is a great *preventive* measure for bad smells under the toilet.

A sign that should be hung
above every toilet that the male sex uses:
"Our aim is to keep this room clean.
Your aim would be appreciated."

MORE BATHROOM TIPS

Soapdishes. To clean, soak in boiling water and scrub with an SOS or stainless-steel pad. To prevent them from becoming a problem in the future, spray with a vegetable cooking spray like Pam or put a layer of plastic wrap on the bottom of the dish.

Curling tile by bathtub. Lay a throw rug next to the tub and let the edge climb up the side about two inches. The water will run down the rug instead of under the tile. Caulk the tile at the edge of the bathtub so water cannot run underneath it and destroy the subfloor.

Small children. To prevent small children from locking themselves in the bathroom, throw a towel over the door so it can't shut fully.

Bath mats. Wash them in the washing machine with towels and hang them out to dry. Do not put them in a dryer.

Nonslip bathroom strips. To whiten stained strips on the bottom of the bathtub, scrub them with a solution of $\frac{1}{2}$ cup turpentine and 2 tablespoons salt.

YOUR NOTES & CLEANING RECIPES

_____

_____

_____

_____

_____

_____

_____

_____

_____

_____

_____

_____

_____

_____

_____

_____

_____

_____

5 Kitchens

It has been said that the kitchen is the heart of the home. If this is true, most homes are suffering from mild heartburn while a lot of others are close to cardiac arrest. There are several things that can make an antiseptically clean kitchen look dirty:

1. **FLOORS.** The areas under the sink and highchair become sticky and dull long before the rest of the kitchen floor needs scrubbing. Save energy and time and keep the floor beautiful by putting throw rugs in these two places.

2. **CUPBOARD DOORS AND DRAWERS.** When they are left swinging open, they are not only a hazard but make the rest of the kitchen look disorganized.

3. **WASHRAG TRACKS.** Many women do not wipe off the counter, table, and appliances after they wash them. This not only causes the finishes to become dull, but it leaves washrag tracks that stick out like a woman in her ninth month of pregnancy.

4. **CLUTTER.** Clear it out! Take last year's PTA notices and wedding invitations off the bulletin board. Try to put the keys, newspaper, telephone book, mail, etc., where they can't be seen. Maybe you could even find another convenient place for some of those convenience appliances that make it so inconvenient to find counterspace to work on.

A really big problem for many women is kitchen "lonelyitis." Believe me, I know just how the Mormon pioneers felt when they watched helplessly as a swarm of crickets marched through their crops, leaving only stubble and ruin behind. I have seen similar destruction in my kitchen. Many meals that take hours to prepare take only minutes to eat and seconds for everyone to disappear out of dish range, leaving poor Mom alone with bones, scraps, dirty dishes—and the blues.

It is great to teach our little ones to say thank you, but it is even greater to teach them to show their gratitude by helping with the work. Children can be taught how to cook as soon as they know how to read and they can be taught to help with the dishes much earlier. Very small children can take their plates to the sink or dishwasher. Older children can work as a team to do the dishes. To avoid conflict, give each one a specific task to complete. Rotate assignments periodically so that by the time they are preteens or teenagers they can do a thorough job in the kitchen all by themselves. "Many hands make light work" may be an old saying, but it is still good advice for a mother with an attack of lonelyitis.

The honeymoon is over when he phones
that he'll be late for supper and she has already
left a note that it's in the refrigerator.
—Bill Lawrence

COUNTERS

PLASTIC LAMINATE SHEETING (FORMICA)

There are two different finishes on Formica counters: slick Formica (it is shiny or glossy) and dull Formica (such as the butcher-block or leather-grain look). For general care, both can be washed with a damp rag and wiped dry. Never put cleanser on Formica, because it will scratch the surface and eventually take off the finish.

Most stains can be removed by squeezing a fresh lemon over the stain. Let it soak for about $1/2$ hour, then sprinkle some baking soda over the lemon juice. Scrub it with a terry cloth rag, rinse, and wipe dry.

Kool-Aid and other powdered drink mixes, grape juice, and Jell-O are the hardest stains to get out of Formica. Most of the time the lemon will take these stains out, but it is best to prevent them. Put a paper towel or napkin under the bottles or cans. Mix the drinks and Jell-O in the sink instead of on the counter or put a towel under the pitcher or bowl. Ink marks from frozen food cans can usually be removed with Thoro (page 13) or the juice of a lemon.

Slick Formica is a beautiful counter to keep up. I like to use lemon oil on it about once a week. Put the lemon oil on a rag and rub it into the counter, then use another rag and wipe it dry. This cleans the counter and puts a beautiful shine on it, too.

Dull Formica is much harder to care for than slick Formica and it loses its beauty much faster if it is not properly cleaned. For best cleaning results, pour undiluted club soda (stocked by most grocery stores) directly on the counter. Wash, rinse with warm water, and wipe it dry. Club soda can also be used to take out stains on dull Formica. To brighten it, use a white low-luster cream like Johnson's Jubilee Cleaner. Put it on a rag, wipe the counter, and rub it dry.

Another good reducing exercise consists
in placing both hands against the table edge and pushing back.
—Robert Quillen

WHITE TILE

Pour liquid bleach on the counter and scrub with a nylon brush. Let it soak for about an hour and then rinse and wipe dry. Do this quite often so that the grout between the tiles doesn't get grimy or collect built-up dirt.

COLORED TILE

Pour water over the surface of the counter. Scatter drops of dish soap on top of the water. Scrub with a nylon brush, rinse, and wipe dry.

If the grout needs to be whitened, use liquid bleach or white toothpaste on a toothbrush or nylon scrub brush and scour.

BUTCHER BLOCK (WOOD)

If you are remodeling your kitchen or building a new house, I recommend that you have a butcher block put next to the stove. Hot food can be taken out of the oven and placed on this surface without any harm to the wood. Formica counter tops that are near the oven and stove are often ruined by hot pans.

Like any natural wood, butcher block needs to be oiled to retain its beautiful shine and to prevent it from drying out and cracking. If food is prepared on it, use mineral or vegetable oil. If food is not prepared on it, then use linseed oil, lemon oil, or the oil that is sold especially for butcher block. The top needs to be oiled about once a month. The bottom also needs oil, but not as frequently. Three times a year is sufficient. Wipe the oil on with a terrycloth rag, let it soak into the butcher block for at least half an hour, and then rub it dry.

Clean the butcher block with a damp cloth or a cloth dipped in vegetable oil, then wipe it dry immediately. To get stains out, use a fresh lemon. Squeeze it on the stain, let it soak for about twenty minutes, then wipe it dry. Stains can also be removed by sanding the wood.

If the surface becomes rough and crisscrossed with knife cuts, it is easy for tiny bits of food to become embedded in it. Other food prepared on the block may then pick up bacteria from trapped, decaying foods, and this presents the danger of salmonella, or food poisoning. Keep the surface smooth by sanding it occasionally.

Reducing: Wishful shrinking.

CABINETS

Murphy's Oil Soap is the best cleaner for metal, painted, imitation wood, Formica, and plastic kitchen cabinets. It is mild on the finish but tough on the dirt. It will also clean real wood, but for that I prefer using a wood-cleaning formula made up of 2 tablespoons boiled linseed oil, 2 tablespoons turpentine, and 1 quart boiling water. Mix the linseed oil and turpentine together in a shortening can or small bucket, then add the boiling water. Make sure that the bucket or can is disposable, because the smell will not come out. Wearing rubber gloves, dip a rag in the cleaner and wring it out well. Do not try to do the whole cabinet at one time. Wash one surface, such as the door, and wipe dry. When the cleaner cools off, the oil and turpentine will separate from the water. Throw it out and make a new batch; don't try to reheat it. I like this formula because the turpentine removes the dirt and greasy finger marks and the linseed oil gives the cabinet a beautiful finish.

Greasy finger smudges around the handles can be removed with a bar of Lava soap. Rub the soap on a wet rag, then scrub. If the stain is really tough, rub the Lava on a wet Scotch Brite pad, scrub, rinse, and wipe dry. After using a Scotch Brite, touch up the wood surface on light-colored cabinets, such as oak and pecan, with Old English Scratch Cover for Light and Medium Wood or Howard's Feed 'N Wax. For darker woods, such as walnut, use Old English Scratch Cover for Dark Wood (pages 11 and 12).

If the area around the handles becomes sticky to the touch, use mineral-spirits paint thinner to clean it and your cupboards will look almost brand-new.

SHELF LINERS

Smooth indoor/outdoor carpet scraps make good shelf liners. (Do not use the rough, grass-looking type.) They keep pans and canned goods from making those ugly black marks on the shelves, and protect the pans from scratches too. Carpet is also good in the silverware drawer, lid drawer, and under the sink.

Contact paper is a little tricky to use as a shelf liner. Most people just follow the directions that come with it. They measure it, strip off the protective backing, and press it flat to the shelf. The bugs love it. It makes such a nice, dark, cozy nest for them to crawl under and lay their eggs. If you already have contact paper on your shelves, pull it back and check for wiggly things. To remove contact paper, soak it with boiling water and scrape with a knife or a spatula. This job is as hard and tedious as trying to strip yellowed wax off a floor.

The correct way to use contact paper is to measure it for the shelf and then strip off about $1\frac{1}{2}$ inches of the backing around all the edges. leave the main part of the backing in the middle. Fit the paper to the shelf and press down the edges. When it is time to change the paper, it will come off very easily.

Scraps of Walltex or wallpaper make a good shelf liner. Make sure it is strippable if you decide to paste it down. A lot of wallpaper is prepasted, so it is as easy to use as commercial shelf paper.

GREASE SPLATTERS

In many kitchens there is a problem of grease from the frying pan, batter from the eggbeater, etc., popping up and making a mess on the underside of the cabinet that hangs over the counter. A sheet of contact paper tacked in this area will act as a splash guard. Apply the contact paper in the same way that you would to a shelf: measure it, strip off $1\frac{1}{2}$ inches of the backing on all the edges, leaving the backing in the middle, and then press it under the cabinet. If the underside of the cabinet can be seen while sitting at the table, make sure that the contact paper matches the kitchen decor. To retain the natural look of the cabinet, clear contact paper may be used. Strip off all the backing, but just tack down the edges to the cabinet. Do not press down the middle. When company comes or the contact paper gets really dirty, pull it off and replace it with another piece.

———————

The wife who drives from the back seat is
no worse than the husband who cooks from the dining-room table.

———————

SINKS

Colored Porcelain. Colored porcelain sinks should never have any bleaching agents put in them. They will fade and dull the color. If the sink is stained, clean it with white vinegar. Pour it over the stain and scrub with a Scotch Brite pad (see page 17).

White Porcelain. For general cleaning, I still prefer good old cleanser. On stains, use liquid bleach. Pour it over the stain, then cover it with a white terry cloth rag or several layers of white paper towels. Pour more bleach over the rag or towels and let it stand for several hours. Rinse out the sink and wipe it dry.

If the entire sink needs a good whitening, pour enough bleach in the sink to barely cover the bottom. Fill the sink with cold water and let it soak overnight or at least eight hours. Also use this bleach method to remove hard-water stains on rubber-coated or plastic dish drainers and trays. Be careful if there are small children in the house. Do this after they go to bed and clean it up before they get up in the morning.

———————

Thank God for dirty dishes,
They have their tales to tell;
While other folks go hungry,
We're eating very well.

Stainless Steel. The best way to keep water spots off a stainless steel sink is to always wipe it out after using it. To remove water spots, use white vinegar or rubbing alcohol as a cleaner, then to put the shine back in the sink, rub it with a rag soaked with club soda and wipe the sink dry. On special occasions I like to use lemon oil, because it leaves a beautiful finish. Put it on a clean rag, scrub, and wipe dry.

CLOGGED DRAINS

For drains clogged with grease or soap residue (this will not remove really tight clogs or drains stopped up with hair), pour ½ cup salt, ½ cup baking soda, and ½ cup vinegar down the drain. Follow this with 2 quarts (or more) of boiling water.

Keep your words soft and sweet;
you never know when you will have to eat them.

LARGE APPLIANCES

In the old days of recipe books,
Papa came home and asked, "What cooks?"
Now, when hunger pangs are gnawing,
He walks in and says, "What's thawing?"

Many of the new kitchen appliances on the market are like a darling little puppy in a pet store. It looks so cute and cuddly in the window, but there is always a degree of disillusionment when you get it home and it messes all over the carpet. Many appliances look great in the store, but they are cleaning nightmares when you get them home.

Buy simple! Fancy dials and gadgets are seldom used. They cost more money to buy and to repair and they are a headache to clean. Even the glass panel on an oven door is hard to keep up. If you follow the recipe and set a timer, there usually isn't a need to constantly peek in the oven.

When buying a new appliance, make sure that every part is easy to clean. Some new refrigerators do not have removable drawers. It is very hard to wipe up spills that leak behind or under a permanent drawer. If milk or meat blood gets under this area, it spoils and really stinks. Some stove tops have the same problem. A boilover is almost impossible to clean up, because there is no way to get under the burners. Buy a stove that has a hinged top or that has reflector pans that lift out or lift up.

---

*An adult is one who has ceased
to grow vertically but not horizontally.*

Colors are also very important to a clean look. The dark colors like avocado, red, brown, and the new dark-tinted glass fronts make good showcases for every little fingerprint and smudge. Light colors stay much cleaner looking because the fingerprints don't show up.

Rough finishes, like the leather look, are really pretty for a while, but dirt and grime are almost impossible to remove if they are allowed to collect.

When shopping for appliances, watch out for those that cannot have any kind of cleaner used on the exterior surface, and avoid buying them. You cannot keep dirt and grease out of the kitchen. When the appliances look bad, the whole kitchen looks terrible.

The exterior surfaces of most large appliances (range, dishwasher, refrigerator, etc.) are made out of a baked-on porcelain enamel. Cleansers and other harsh commercial cleaners will scratch and dull this surface. An SOS pad can be used to scrub off caked-on dirt if you are careful. For everyday cleaning, I like a homemade formula of 2 tablespoons nonsudsy ammonia, 1 teaspoon liquid dish soap, 1 pint rubbing alcohol, and 1 gallon water. For convenience, always keep some in a spray bottle. It is great for washing off dirt and fingerprints on woodwork and walls, too.

When the appliances need an extra shine, use liquid Johnson's Jubilee cleaner. Put it on a soft, damp rag, rub it on, and wipe it dry.

DISHWASHER

For hard-water stains or hard-water buildup: (1) Wet the stain. (2) Sprinkle an orange-flavor powdered instant breakfast drink (any brand— it's the citric acid that does the work) over the stain. (3) Let it stand for one hour. (4) Load the dishes, add the dishwasher detergent, and run it through a normal cycle.

If you are having trouble with spotting on your dishes or glasses, then add 1/2 teaspoon of orange powdered instant breakfast drink to the dishwasher detergent every time you wash the dishes. This will eliminate most of the spotting and make the glasses sparkle.

Sometimes the hard water will leave spots that cling to the glassware through repeated washings. These stains can usually be removed by scrubbing with an SOS pad dipped in hot vinegar.

REFRIGERATOR AND FREEZER

To clean underneath the refrigerator or freezer without pulling it out, take a yardstick and secure an old stocking over it with a rubber band. Swish it under the appliance. This will knock out a lot of the lint and junk that collects there.

The refrigerator and freezer should be pulled out about four times a

61

year and the area underneath given a good scrubbing. At the same time, clean off the condenser coils. These may be found in the back or the bottom of the appliance. Unplug the refrigerator. Using a refrigerator coil brush that can be purchased in appliance stores, brush off the coils, then sweep out the gray fuzzy matter that has dropped. A vacuum may also be used. This will save cleaning up the floor, but it isn't as effective as the brush for cleaning the coils. Keeping the coils clean will make the refrigerator or freezer run smoother and will add years to its life.

Just before you do the grocery shopping is a good time to get rid of all the moldy delicacies in the refrigerator. If you don't have a garbage disposal, then clean out the refrigerator the day the garbage man is coming.

Put paper towels in the bottom of the vegetable and meat drawers. They will collect the dirt and absorb the meat juices.

When washing out the interior, use 3 tablespoons of Murphy's Oil Soap to 2 quarts hot water. For absorbing smells, I use kitty litter. It works much better than baking soda. Put it in a jar or can, or if you don't want anyone to suspect, dump out the traditional box of baking soda and refill it with kitty litter. Remember! If you would clean out your refrigerator every week, you would never have to use a deodorizer!

Freezers should be cleaned out at least once a year. Go through it and put the oldest food on the first shelf (or on top in a chest freezer) so that it will get used up first.

The wonderful world of home appliances now makes
it possible to cook indoors with charcoal and outdoors with gas.
—Bill Vaughan

RANGES
Continuous-Cleaning and Self-Cleaning Ovens. Follow the
manufacturer's instructions. Never use any kind of cleaning aid in a

continuous-cleaning or self-cleaning oven. If the finish is once taken off, the oven won't clean at all, and then it is really a mess.

Sometimes a continuous-cleaning oven will get so that it is not doing the job. Fill a dripper pan full with water and put it in the oven for twenty minutes at 400°F. This will sometimes help to reactivate the continuous-cleaning element.

For grease spots on the window, put the oven door down and coat it with a thin layer of lemon oil. Let this set for an hour to loosen the grease. Scrub with an SOS pad or stainless-steel pad. Make sure all the oil is washed off or the oven will smoke the next time it is used. Wipe dry to prevent streaking.

The continuous-cleaning or self-cleaning features on an oven will not clean the racks and sometimes it causes them to turn blue. To clean the racks, see instructions on page 65. If the racks won't slide easily, a result of leaving them in at high self-cleaning temperatures, apply a little vegetable oil on the runners.

Conventional Oven. I seldom use commercial oven cleaners. Labels on these cleaners caution you not to get them near the nose, eyes, or mouth or any other part of the skin, because the lye and nitrogen compounds will cause burns. Most oven cleaners are dangerous so if you insist on using them, be smart and protect yourself. Wear goggles, rubber gloves, and a face mask. Make sure your kitchen is well ventilated. Open all the doors and windows and never let your children in the room while using an oven cleaner. Even the fumes are dangerous to inhale. Don't buy scented oven cleaners, because you may be tempted to sniff at them. Buy one that smells ghastly so that you will spray and run. Never get the oven cleaner on electrical connections, heating elements, the thermostat, or anything aluminum. It could damage them. Buy a cleaner with a molded finger guide so that you won't accidently point the spray the wrong way and drench yourself. There are a few oven cleaners on the market that do not contain lye. Look for them.

If the oven is mildly dirty, put a small glass bowl of ammonia in the oven at night, then wipe it out the next morning. If there is a spill, immediately pour salt on it. When the oven cools, brush off the burnt food.

"Mildly dirty" ovens are usually found in homes where the family always eats out or where most of the cooking is done in a microwave. If your oven looks like a coal miner's paradise, then it needs a stiffer remedy. Pour lemon ammonia over the crud on the bottom of the oven. If the oven is gas, make sure the ammonia doesn't go down the holes. Take an old terrycloth rag and wipe the whole interior, including the door. Close the door and let the fumes work on the dirt for two or three hours. Scrub out the oven with an SOS pad or stainless-steel pad, then rinse and wipe dry. If the crud is really burned on and won't come off using this method, you will have to use an oven cleaner once, and from then on you can keep the oven clean using this method.

To prevent the oven from getting in bad shape again, spend a few extra dollars and buy some Oven 'N Grill Coating from Amway or Oven Spray from Fuller Brush. Spray the inside of the oven and shut it up for another hour. This also puts out some obnoxious fumes, but it makes future spills much easier to wipe off.

Finally, dampen the floor of the oven and smooth down a piece of aluminum foil on it, dull side up. Place several shorter pieces of foil in the center of the first sheet, so that if there is a spill, the top sheet can be lifted off and there is another one waiting and ready. **DO NOT LET THE FOIL TOUCH THE OVEN BURNER!** To check this, bend down so your eyes are level with the burner.

I'm sorry for people, wherever they are,
Who live in a house with no cookie jar.

The grease spots on the window usually come off with the ammonia method and the help of an SOS pad. If they do not, coat the window with lemon oil and let it set for an hour. Scrub with an SOS pad, rinse thoroughly, and wipe dry. Sometimes moisture collects between the double glass on the oven door. I don't know of any way to get that out. Whatever you do, don't take the oven door apart. I tried that once and it took me five hours to get it all back together. The glass and the insulation have to be put back in perfect order so the stove doesn't leak heat.

Racks. Most people seldom use both of the racks that come with the oven. Remove one rack, store it, and use it when needed. It would eliminate half of a dirty cleaning chore. Oven racks (reflector pans and rings from the stove top) can be cleaned in the bathtub. Place a large bath towel on the bottom of the tub to keep it from getting scratched. Add 1/4 cup of ammonia to just enough steaming hot water to cover the racks. Let them soak for two or three hours and then scrub them with an SOS or stainless-steel pad.

Another method is to place the racks (reflector pans and rings from the stove top) in a large plastic garbage bag. Spray with ammonia, then drape a towel over them and pour a little ammonia on top of the towel. Seal the bag for at least an hour. Rinse in the bathtub or use the garden hose. If the rings and reflector pans are still dirty, dip an SOS pad or stainless-steel pad in a silver cream, such as Mrs. Wright's, and scrub.

———

There is one thing more exasperating
than a wife who can cook and won't and that's a
wife who can't cook and will.
—Robert Frost

———

Broiler. Really cruddy broiler pans can be cleaned using the technique outlined for electric frying pans on page 69. If food has been burned on, they will have to be sprayed with oven cleaner and placed in the oven for several hours. Wash them thoroughly, rinse, and wipe dry.

After cleaning, spray the broiler pans with a cooking oil like Pam and then line them with aluminum foil. The rack can also be lined if slits are made in the foil where the holes in the rack are. After using the broiler pan, remove the foil, wash in hot soapy water and reline. This will save hours of work and it is especially great in keeping new broiler pans from getting stained.

Murphy's law: When a broken appliance is demonstrated
for the repairman, it will work perfectly.

Stove Tops. Remove the rings around the burner and the reflector pans (the tin bowl under the burner) and place them in the ammonia bath or garbage sack with the racks. Soak the surface under the burners with $1/8$ cup of Spic and Span, Soilax *or* ammonia to 1 gallon of hot water. Scrub with an SOS pad or stainless-steel pad until the spilled-over crud is loosened, then wipe it out with a clean, dry rag.

To prevent having to do that nasty chore again, dampen the surface under the burners and put a layer of aluminum foil all across the area. Pat it down so that it will lie flat. Because part of the messy spills are boilovers which leave an abundance of liquid under the stove, place throw-away aluminum pie tins under each burner to catch the spill. These can be taken out and washed and used again and again. This, of course, is not possible in a gas range because of the pipes under the burners. Here you can mold a bowl around the pipes with some aluminum foil to catch the spills.

Scrub the reflector pans and rings (that have been soaking in the ammonia) with an SOS or stainless-steel pad. If the pans won't come clean, purchase new ones in the grocery store. They are fairly inexpensive and universally sized to fit most stove tops. The reflector pans and rings can be put in the oven and sprayed with the Oven 'N Grill Coating or Oven Spray at the same time the rest of the oven is sprayed. This will make it easier to clean them the next time around.

Tip: Grease spots behind the stove top are usually not a problem if they are wiped off immediately, but a lot of us get busy putting dinner on and just forget. Use lemon oil as a cleaner on slick Formica. Put a thin layer on the area and scrub with a stainless-steel pad, or if you don't have that, use an SOS pad. Rinse it off and wipe dry. If you want it to be shiny, then do not rinse off the lemon oil, just rub it dry. Use club soda to clean dull Formica; a soap-filled pad and hot water on paint (this may take off some of the finish); and 1 tablespoon of ammonia to 1 quart hot water and an SOS pad on Walltex.

Clear contact paper is really good behind the stove area to guard the Formica or Walltex from grease splashes. Do not use it on paint or wallpaper. Measure the contact paper and strip off all the backing. Tack down the edges to the Formica or Walltex, but do not press down the middle. When the contact paper looks greasy, just peel it off and replace it. Your Formica or Walltex will always look like new. Or buy a piece of Plexiglas—the type sold for cutting boards—and put it behind the stove top.

Microwaves. Always follow the manufacturer's suggestions for cleaning a microwave oven. Clean out after each use with soapy water and wipe dry. For stubborn spots, use an SOS pad.

SMALL APPLIANCES

Food processors, juicers, mixers, and the like are easiest to clean immediately after use. Do not let the food dry on them. *Unplug the appliance,* remove detachable parts from the motor section, disassemble, and place in a dishpan with hot, soapy water. Most appliance parts should not be washed in a dishwasher. Cutting blades should not be allowed to soak in the water because it dulls the cutting edge, so rinse them immediately and wipe them dry. An SOS or stainless-steel pad can be used to remove stubborn food.

Place a towel on the counter next to the sink and put the motor section on a towel. Scrub the motor section with a damp, hot, soapy rag and wipe it dry. *Do not get water in electrical parts or immerse motor section in water.* Remove stubborn stains with an SOS pad. Use a percolator brush or other narrow brush to get into hard-to-reach places. Rinse and then wipe dry.

BLENDER

Fill the blender half-full with water and add a few drops of liquid dish soap. Turn it on for a few seconds. Rinse the blender thoroughly and turn it upside down to dry.

CAN OPENER

Most of the new electric can openers have removable blades that can be put in soapy water. Make sure the blades are dried thoroughly to prevent rusting.

If the can opener does not have removable blades and it is electric, pull out the plug and scrub the blades with a toothbrush.

To clean the old-fashioned can opener (nonelectric, but attached to the wall), wet a paper towel in soapy water and run it through the blades, then rinse the blades by running through a second paper towel that has been wet with clear water.

GARBAGE DISPOSAL

68   Put ½ cup of vinegar in an ice-cube tray, fill the tray with water, and

freeze. (Be sure to mark it or your family may get an unhappy surprise with their drinks!) Grind the vinegar cubes down the disposal once a week. The ice cubes sharpen the blades and the vinegar cleans and freshens the disposal.

If you come home from a vacation and there is an unwelcome odor in the kitchen, it is usually the garbage disposal that is to blame. Don't wait for the vinegar water to freeze. Turn on the disposal and pour in a cup of vinegar. Rinse immediately by turning on the cold water for a few minutes.

ELECTRIC FRYING PAN

This method will usually clean off all the black, cruddy buildup on the bottom of an electric frying pan. Place the electric frying pan, upside down, inside a plastic garbage bag. Leave the bag open so you can pour ammonia on the back of the pan. (Do not let any ammonia touch the interior of the pan.) Put a terrycloth rag on top of the ammonia, then saturate the rag with more ammonia. Close the bag and seal so it is airtight. Let it soak overnight or for about eight hours. Then remove the bag and run the pan under hot water. For extra-tough spots, scrub with a stainless-steel or SOS pad. This is also a good remedy for the outside barbecue grill. After soaking it with ammonia in sealed bag for eight hours, just rinse it off with the hose.

TOASTER

Wash with soapy water. Do not get water in electrical parts. If necessary, scrub with an SOS pad, and wipe dry.

The best grease is elbow grease.
—*B. C. Forbes*

TOASTER OVEN

If it is mildly dirty, then wash with soapy water. If the inside has baked-on crud, then scrub with ⅛ cup Spic and Span or Soilax to ½ gallon of hot water, or use 1 tablespoon of ammonia to ½ gallon of hot water. An SOS pad will remove stubborn, burned-on food. Rinse out and wipe dry. Spray the interior and the trays with Oven 'N Grill Coating or Oven Spray. This keeps the food from sticking and makes the oven easier to clean the next time.

PANS

If food sticks to any pan, fill it half-full of water and add ¼ cup Spic and Span, baking soda, or dishwasher detergent. Bring to a boil, turn off the heat, and let it stand for about an hour. Use an SOS or stainless-steel pad if it is necessary and if it won't ruin the finish of the pan.

Aluminum. Discolored pans will brighten if highly acidic foods, such as tomatoes or rhubarb, are cooked in them. Vinegar can also be used as a cleaner. Pour in enough to cover the stained area. Bring it to a boil, turn down the heat, and let it simmer for five minutes. Let it soak in the pan for an hour after the burner is turned off and then wash the pan.

Brass. Worcestershire sauce will polish brass. Put it directly on the pan, scrub it with an SOS pad, rinse, and wipe dry.

There is a new Chinese diet:
eat all you want, but use one chopstick.

Copper. Ketchup polishes copper. Pour it on and rub with an SOS pad. A lemon half dipped in salt can also be used. Rub it all over the copper and rinse. For stains, put toothpaste on a damp SOS pad and scrub.

Enamelware. If food sticks to the bottom of the pan, add 3 tablespoons of baking soda to just enough boiling water to cover the bottom of the pan. Let it soak for an hour.

Iron. A little salt and vinegar boiled in the pan will loosen burned-on food. If it gets really bad, then it can be cleaned like an electric fry pan (see page 69).

Iron pans should always be coated with grease after each wash to recondition them and to prevent rusting.

Nonstick Pans. To remove stains and baked-on food from Teflon, SilverStone, etc., put enough water in the pan to cover the stain and then add ⅛ cup of dishwashing soap. Bring the water to a boil and let it simmer for fifteen minutes. Wash the pan thoroughly, rinse, and wipe dry. Recondition the pan by applying a coating of shortening or vegetable oil.

---

*More people commit suicide
with a fork than with any other weapon.*

Stainless Steel. Pour white vinegar on the stain and scrub it with an SOS or stainless-steel pad.

Other Metal Pans. A stain will come off a pie, cake, or bread pan if a raw onion is rubbed over it. (Put salt on your hands afterwards to get the onion smell out.) To remove rust, use a raw potato dipped in cleanser. Rub it over the rust and rinse.

Pyrex. To remove baked-on food, soak the Pyrex for at least twenty minutes in hot, soapy water, then scrub with an SOS pad. Pyrex is dishwasher safe, but baked-on foods need to be removed before washing.

Teakettle. Fill the teakettle with equal parts of vinegar and water. Bring it to a boil, turn off the heat, and let it stand overnight. This will remove the lime deposits left from hard water.

Thermos Bottle. Fill the bottle with hot water and add 1 tablespoon of baking soda. Let it soak overnight.

KITCHEN TOOLS

Cutting Board. To remove onion or garlic smells, slice a lime and rub it into the board. Clean stains with a sliced lemon.

Garlic Press. Clean and remove the smell by rubbing it with bread. Rinse and wipe dry.

Grater. Brush off any clinging food with a pastry brush and wash in soapy water. Never put the grater in a dishwasher or let it stand in water because it will rust and the blades will become dull.

Plastic. For stains and yellowing, scrub with a damp rag that has been dipped in baking soda.

Sponges. Wash them in the washing machine with the towels. To recondition them, soak in 2 tablespoons salt and 2 quarts water then wash.

SOS and Other Soap-Filled Pads. Store them in a clay pot to prevent them from rusting.

---

*Housework is what women do
that nobody notices until they don't do it.*

MORE KITCHEN TIPS

Scales. Test them by weighing a five- or ten-pound bag of sugar.

China Storage. Put a paper plate between each plate. This prevents

scratching and also keeps plates from getting dusty.

Wax. Use a hair dryer to remove candle drippings from a counter top, tabletop, or other flat surfaces. Blow the wax until it softens, then use a paper towel or napkin to wipe it up.

---

*Very few people alive today seem to recall
the evening Adam came stomping
into Eve's kitchen to complain, "Confound it,
you've put my pants in the salad again!"*

Garbage Cans. Buy a kitchen garbage can the same size as the grocery bags you bring home from the store. Use the bags to line the garbage can instead of buying plastic liners.

Vinyl Chairs. To cover splits on the seats and backs of vinyl kitchen chairs, apply bathtub appliques, the kind that are used in the bottom of tubs to prevent slippage. They come in many pretty shapes and colors.

YOUR NOTES & CLEANING RECIPES

6 Carpets

Carpets are bought by the yard and worn by the foot.
—A. R. Spofford

When buying new carpets, keep in mind that they are good foot wipers. I worked for a doctor who put a six-inch-thick white shag in every room of his house. It made me tired to just walk through it. They had to build up the piano so that they could use the pedals, and they bought an expensive vacuum with a motorized handle because their upright vacuum buckled. Before long the carpet around the heater vents was gray and the traffic areas were dark and dingy and matted down. After a few years they ripped it out.

Most of us can't afford an expensive mistake like that. Yellow, orange, and light-blue carpets show all the dirt. They never look clean. Whites and off-whites are terrible. The dark, solid colors show lint really badly, but I would rather contend with that than put up with dirty traffic areas. The multicolored carpets don't show either dirt or lint.

VACUUMING

Carpets need to be vacuumed several times a week if they get heavy traffic. When they are walked on, the dirt gets ground into the carpet and cuts the fibers. This is one of the reasons there is so much lint in the vacuum bag.

Choose a good vacuum cleaner for your carpet, but be wise about it.

75

One of my friends bought an expensive vacuum from a door-to-door salesman. Her apartment only had a throw rug.

Don't worry about the dozens of attachments that go along with the vacuum. You'll probably never use the head massager or the spray-paint adapter. Just be sure that you have the basics. You will need the round brush for vents, lampshades, louver doors, venetian blinds, and the baseboards; the crevice tool (long, thin attachment) for deep upholstery cleaning and cleaning around the upholstery buttons and in corners; the four-inch upholstery brush for stairs, drapes, and surface upholstery cleaning; and the linoleum brush for vacuuming uncarpeted floors.

CLEANING

Do not shampoo a new carpet until it is absolutely necessary. There is a protective coating on most new carpets. Some coatings permanently resist stains, but many are washed away with the first shampoo. After the first shampoo, the carpet will get dirtier much faster and it will have to be cleaned more often.

When cleaning a carpet, don't move couches, chairs, pianos, or other heavy furniture. It doesn't get dirty under those areas.

The method of carpet cleaning that I like best doesn't use a commercial shampoo. As a matter of fact, you won't even need to rent or buy a carpet shampooer, so think of all the money that can be saved!

Mix together in a bucket ½ cup of ammonia, ½ cup cleaning solvent (see page 12), and ½ gallon warm water. If the carpets are really dirty add ½ cup Spic and Span to this cleaning solution. (*No,* this will not gas you, or I would have been dead thirty years ago!) For low-pile carpets use old bath towels. Use a nylon brush for shag carpets. Don't use a bristle brush or you will be picking bristles out of the carpet forever. Now get down on hands and knees so you are close enough to the carpet to see the bad dirt spots (you need the exercise anyway). Dip the brush or towel in the ammonia and cleaning-solvent solution and scrub one section at a time.

A section would be about four feet by four feet. Before going on, rinse that section with 1 cup of white vinegar mixed with 1 gallon of warm water. Mix this in a second bucket, soak a towel with the vinegar rinse, and scrub the area just washed. Use another towel to wipe it as dry as possible. Go on to the next section and do it the same way.

I have worked with all kinds of commercial cleaners and shampooers, but I have found this method to be the best. It sounds like a lot of work, but actually it is less. The carpets will look bright and beautiful. Ammonia and the cleaning solvent really remove the dirt. The vinegar brightens the carpet and takes out any cleaner residue, so the carpet will stay cleaner-looking longer.

There is always a lot to be thankful for
if you take time to look for it.
Right now I am sitting here thinking how nice
it is that wrinkles don't hurt.
—James Holt McGrawran

COMMERCIAL SHAMPOOS

Now, I don't for one minute think that I will convert everyone into cleaning carpets my way, so for those who love to use carpet shampooers, steam cleaners, and the like, add a few years to the carpet's life by rinsing the soap out immediately after shampooing. I know that the shampoo manufacturers don't say anything about this, but what do you think happens to all that soap that is being brushed into the carpet? The vacuum cleaner won't remove it. If soap is left in the carpet it will break down the fibers. If this is happening to your carpet, you will notice a lot of carpet fiber in the vacuum or you may even see places in the carpet that are beginning to mat down or turn to fuzz. The soap also attracts dirt and in a couple of weeks of foot traffic you will be wondering what happened

77

to the hard work that you put into scrubbing that carpet.

To rinse off a carpet that has been washed with a commercial shampoo, add 1 cup of white vinegar to 1 gallon of lukewarm water. Rinse one section at a time and wipe it dry as you go. Change the vinegar water frequently because it will get quite sudsy and you don't want to rub that back into the carpet.

Even a tombstone says good things about a fellow who is down!

Tip: When shampooing, slip a plastic sandwich bag under each leg of the furniture to prevent water damage.

KITCHEN CARPETS

If you can possibly help yourself, don't ever buy a carpet with a black backing. These carpets sometimes have the brighter, more enticing colors and they are usually cheaper, but they are really hard to keep clean. Don't choose a solid-color carpet for the kitchen. The light ones show the dirt and the dark ones show the spills. A medium-colored, multicolored, or patterned carpet is the best. If a stain gets on one of these, it just blends in with the carpet. I also like a short, medium-colored or multicolored shag in the kitchen. It doesn't show the dirt.

There are times when if you are not feeling like yourself,
it is quite an improvement.

Use the same method for cleaning carpets that I have just described, but make sure the rag is only slightly damp when washing or rinsing. Kitchen carpets should never have a lot of water put on them, because many of them have black backings and the black will bleed through the carpet.

THROW RUGS

When throw rugs look lightly soiled, shake them out well, then put them in the dryer on air-fluff with a wet towel. This will brighten the rug and make it last longer between washings.

Never use hot water on throw rugs. It makes the rubber backing peel. In the final rinse add ½ cup white vinegar. This brightens the rugs and breaks down the soap that will otherwise stay in the carpet fiber. Let the rug line-dry and then fluff it up by putting it through the air-fluff cycle in the dryer for a few minutes.

Limp rugs can be restored by brushing several coats of shellac or strong liquid starch over the back. Let the rug dry thoroughly before putting it back on the floor.

Work is the greatest thing in the world,
so we should always save some of it for tomorrow.
—Don Herold

SPECIAL PROBLEMS

Lint. Lint is very hard to remove with a vacuum cleaner in many places. In a large bucket, pour ½ cup ammonia and 1 gallon of water. Dip a broom in the bucket and sweep off the lint around the baseboards. Use a whiskbroom for hard-to-reach places like behind the toilet and in tight corners.

Indentations. To raise the nap on a carpet or rug that has been flattened or matted down by heavy furniture, hold a steam iron just above the flattened area. Make sure the iron doesn't touch the carpet. The steam from the iron will raise the nap.

Carpet deodorizer. To deodorize a medium-sized room, sprinkle 1 cup of baking soda evenly over the entire carpet surface. Wait thirty minutes, then vacuum it up. This will absorb smoking, cooking, and pet odors, if they are not stale or old. It will give a room a fresher, cleaner smell. Do *not* put baking soda on a damp carpet.

Dust. Much of the dust in carpets, drapes, and furniture can be cut down by changing the air filter in the furnace quite often. Heating floor vents or registers can also be covered with cheesecloth. It is very porous and will not hinder the flow of heat and air. Take the vent off and tape a piece of cheesecloth across the back. The cheesecloth should be washed when it gets dirty and dusty.

No matter what your lot in life,
be sure you build something on it.

STAINS AND SPILLS

A prewash laundry soil-and-stain remover such as Spray 'n Wash makes a good spot remover for some spills. So does shaving cream. Spray or squirt it on, work it into the spill, rinse with vinegar and water and wipe dry.

A cheaper spot remover is a mixture of 1 teaspoon white vinegar in 1 quart of warm water. This works well on butter, coffee, gravy, and chocolate that is spilled on either carpet or upholstery. Sponge up as much of the liquid as possible, or if the spill is solid, scrape it off the surface or the material. Then dampen the rag with the vinegar-and-water solution and scrub the spot. Let the surface dry. Repeat if necessary, and finish by vacuuming over the area.

Murphy's Law: The chance of a piece of bread
falling with the buttered side down
is directly proportional to the cost of the carpet.

Animal Stains. Blot up the excess moisture with paper towels. Pour white vinegar on the spot and continue blotting up the moisture. Lay a dry towel over the stain, put a heavy object (like a brick) on it, and leave it overnight.

Blood. Follow the directions for using vinegar and water as a spot remover, but before vacuuming, rub the spot with a rag dipped in a cleaning solvent.

Cigarette Burns. Scrape off as much of the burn as possible and wash with vinegar and water.

Faded or Bleached Spots. Bleached spots are usually found in the laundry area or around the toilet, where bleach or toilet-bowl cleaner has accidently spilled or splashed. Animal urine will also bleach a carpet. If the spot is small, then color it with a permanent magic marker that is the same color as the carpet. For larger areas, such as by the sliding glass doors where the sun has faded the carpet, the carpet will have to be dyed. In a bucket mix together 1 cup of ammonia, 1 cup cleaning solvent, ½ gallon warm water, and a bottle of liquid Rit clothes dye that matches the carpet. Scrub this into the carpet, rinse it with vinegar and water to set the dye, and wipe dry (see Carpet Rinse, page 78).

Foul Smells. Cat or dog urine is the hardest kind of smell to get out of a carpet. Sometimes undiluted vinegar will neutralize the odor. Liquid

Lysol Brand Disinfectant is also good. Pour 2 tablespoons of the Lysol into ½ gallon of water and scrub the area. Another method is to pour a four-ounce bottle of lemon extract in two quarts of water and scrub it in. Do not rinse any of these deodorizers out, but wipe them as dry as possible. The Lysol method and the lemon extract method are also good for urine smells around the toilet.

If the urine smell persists after you've tried these methods, then it has soaked into the padding. The carpet will have to be pulled up and the stained portion of the padding replaced.

Glue. Fresh glue can be scraped off with a dull knife or washed off with a damp soapy cloth. If the glue is hard then carefully apply drops of hot white vinegar, cleaning solvent *or* fingernail polish remover (without an oil base) over the glue. Put an absorbent cloth over this and then pour more of the removal agent over the cloth. Place a bowl upside-down over the stain to prevent evaporation. Repeat the process every ten minutes until the glue is soft, then scrape it off using the edge of a spoon or butter knife. Wash the area-with hot water.

Grease Spots. Pour baking soda or cornmeal over the grease and brush it through the pile of the carpet. Leave it overnight, then vacuum it out.

Gum. Put ice cubes on the gum to make it go solid. Scrape up as much as possible with a knife and take out what is left with a cleaning solvent or a prewash laundry soil-and-stain remover.

Kool-Aid or Fla-Vor-Aid. Kool-Aid and Fla-Vor-Aid leave a stain that is impossible to get out of many carpets. I have found that Fels-Naptha, a bar soap that is found near the laundry detergents in the grocery store (see page 11) will sometimes do the job. Wet the carpet and scrub the stain with the soap bar. Rinse out the soap with vinegar and water. Club soda will also work in many cases. Put it on a rag. Scrub the carpet, rinse and wipe dry.

On a white or very light carpet, a stain can be bleached out. The bleach may leave a spot that is whiter than the carpet, so you will have to decide which is worse: a dark colored Kool-Aid stain on a white carpet or a lighter-colored, bleached-out spot. Mix 2 tablespoons bleach with 2 cups water. Scrub a small spot with a toothbrush and a larger spill with a terrycloth rag. Rinse with vinegar and water.

Wax. Scrape off as much as possible. Put a brown paper bag over the wax and run a hot iron over the bag. This acts as a blotter and absorbs the wax.

YOUR NOTES & CLEANING RECIPES

_____

_____

_____

_____

_____

_____

_____

_____

_____

_____

_____

_____

_____

_____

_____

_____

_____

_____

_____

7 Floors

*My wife's idea of housecleaning
is to sweep the room at a glance.
—Joey Adams*

Whenever you go shopping for a new floor, the most important question to ask (after *Can I afford it?*) is *How does it clean and wear?* That beautiful but impractical foot wiper will soon become an irksome enemy if it shows all the dirt or if it is hard to keep up, because the floor gets more dirt and traffic than any cleaning area in your home.

Buy a medium-colored floor. A light floor shows the dirt and a dark floor shows all the footprints. A multicolored floor with a "fun" pattern will hide the dirt and scratches. Knobby or textured floors also hide scuffs and scratches, but they accumulate dirt faster and it is really hard to keep them clean. Stay away from a floor with grooves. Spending the afternoon armed with only a toothpick to attack the food and dirt in tiny cracks is not my idea of a jolly holiday. High-gloss floors keep their looks longer than low-gloss floors.

The new no-wax floors are great, but watch out for cushioned types. They are easier to damage than the uncushioned floors. Chairs and tables may leave indentations, and even dropping plates or glasses on a cushioned floor can mar the finish. You can imagine what a refrigerator will do to this type of floor when it is moved out for cleaning.

The best way to keep any floor beautiful is to keep it clean. A floor needs to be swept or vacuumed often so the dirt doesn't get ground into the wax or finish (see Brooms, page 13). Scrubbing should be part of the weekly routine chores. When washing a floor, move as much of the furniture out of the room as possible. Scrub one small section of the floor at a time. Always wipe that little area dry before going on. It is amazing how much dirt comes off the floor in the wiping process. Wiping also keeps the floor from looking dull, protects the finish or wax, and makes the chore go quicker because you don't have to wait for it to dry. I still prefer getting down on hands and knees to scrub a floor. Besides being a good back exercise, the floor gets much cleaner that way. However, if you are addicted to a mop, put a large, dry terrycloth towel or rag under the mop to wipe the area dry before moving to the next section (see Mops, page 14).

Terry towels make the best floor rags for scrubbing and wiping. A scrub brush is seldom needed except on tile floors or very filthy, grimy floors. Brushes will scratch a waxed surface and ruin a no-wax floor.

God made women without a sense of humor
so that they could love men instead of laugh at them.
—Eagle, *Dothan, Ala.*

Tip: When moving furniture, put old stockings over the legs to prevent them from scratching the floors. This is not particularly esthetic for furniture that is constantly on the move, like kitchen chairs. To prevent chairs from scratching the floor, paint the feet with shellac or rub them with paste floor wax. Clear nail polish is also a good coating.

LINOLEUM

"No-wax" linoleum should never have a harsh cleaner on it. Scrub it with 1 tablespoon white vinegar to 1 gallon warm water.

The old linoleum needs to be waxed fairly often to protect it from water and wear. Many people believe that a floor should be stripped every time it is waxed. This is nonsense. A floor only needs to be stripped when it begins to look dull or when it starts to yellow. This should only happen every five to ten years. If your floor is yellowing much more often, then change waxes. You will pay many times over in extra work for the cheap wax that you are tempted to buy. I have had the best success with Tre-wax or Glo-Coat.

To strip a floor, use ½ cup Spic and Span or Soilax and ½ cup ammonia to 1 gallon very hot water. Work with a small area at a time. Pour the solution on the floor and let it stand for five minutes. Don't let the water dry or the wax will set again, so the process has to be started all over. Scrape the wax off with a Teflon spatula. An SOS or stainless-steel pad will help get into grooves or corners. After stripping, apply three coats of wax to the main traffic areas and one or two coats of wax to the less active areas to build up the shine and protect the floor.

For quick mop-ups, use cold water and wipe dry. This will help to keep the floor shiny between waxes. Just before waxing, scrub the floor well with ¼ cup ammonia, Spic and Span or Soilax, to 1 gallon warm water.

A working girl is one who quit her job to get married.
—E. J. Kiefer

TILE

Never wax a tile floor! After a while the wax will crackle and it is impossible to remove. To scrub, use ¼ cup Spic and Span, Soilax, or ammonia, to a gallon of hot water. A nylon scrub brush is best, because the other types may scratch the floor.

To give the floor a shiny, glazed look, add ½ cup of powdered clothes starch to 1 gallon of warm water. Apply a very thin layer in the same way you would apply wax, and let it dry.

Gray, dirty grout really ruins the beauty of a tile floor. To whiten, pour a small amount of undiluted liquid clothes bleach directly on the floor and scrub with a nylon brush. Rinse with warm water, changing the rinse water frequently. Wipe the area before moving on to the next section of tile.

NO-WAX VINYL

Cleaning agents should never be used (and, we hope, never even accidently spilled) on a vinyl no-wax floor. Dirt usually doesn't stick to the no-wax finish, so it doesn't need a heavy cleaner and since there isn't the problem of wax build up it doesn't need a harsh cleaner. Also, the no-wax shine will last far longer if you use a mild cleaner. I recommend 1 tablespoon of white vinegar to 1 gallon of water. Vinegar is an excellent cleaner for normal dirt build up and it is cheap to use.

It is very important to scrub one small section at a time and wipe it dry before going on. If water isn't wiped off immediately it will eventually ruin the finish and the floor will lose its no-wax shine and look dull all the time.

What the manufacturers and sellers don't tell you is that your no-wax floor will not shine on forever. In fact, many flooring stores sell a vinyl dressing to restore the no-wax finish. These dressings will have to be applied about every three to six months once the original finish has worn off. They are the best remedy for this kind of floor. Avoid a cheap commercial wax. It will make the floor yellow. Glo-Coat and Tre-wax are two very good waxes and either could be used in place of the manufacturer's product, but of course, you will have to start waxing much more frequently if you use these products.

Nothing modernizes a home so completely
as an ad offering it for sale.

SPECIAL REMEDIES

SOS may take the finish off of a no-wax floor, but some stains are impossible to remove without it. On all the problems listed below, try a soft rag first. This applies equally to linoleum, tile, and no-wax vinyl.

Black scuff marks. Dip a terrycloth rag into a cleansing cream, such as Pond's, and scrub. If this doesn't remove the mark, then dip an SOS pad in liquid wax and scrub off the mark. The SOS will remove the mark and the wax will put the shine back on your floor.

Crayon. Scrub with silver polish on a damp rag. The area will have to be rewaxed.

Grease. (Shortening, liquid vegetable oil, turkey drippings, etc.) Put ice cubes on top of the grease and rub it in. This will solidify it and make it easier to wipe up. On a no-wax floor, wash with a few drops of liquid dish soap in 1 gallon of hot water. On tile and linoleum, scrub with 1/4 cup of ammonia, Spic and Span, or Soilax in 1 gallon of water. An SOS pad may be needed to remove all the grease. Rewax the floor.

Tar. Scrape off as much as possible with a knife. Scrub with toothpaste squeezed on an SOS pad.

The fellow that owns his own home
is always just coming out of a hardware store.
—Frank McKinney Hubbard

MARBLE

Wash with a few drops of mild dish soap (such as Joy or Ivory) in 1 gallon of warm water. Rinse with clean warm water and wipe dry. Apply a very thin coat of Johnson's Paste Wax to the floor. This comes in a light or dark color to match the marble. Turtle Wax (white-paste car wax) is also very good for a light-colored or white marble. Let the wax stand for twenty minutes, then hand-buff it. This will help to protect the marble.

Most stains can be removed by applying a thick paste made of household cleanser and hot water. Spread it over the stain and let it dry thoroughly. This will take at least twenty-four hours. The paste can easily be lifted by dampening it slightly. Rinse the area and wipe dry.

WOOD

Wood floors are becoming very popular again. They are beautiful and well worth the extra work involved to care for them. For cleaning purposes, there are two types of floors. The first kind has been varnished, shellacked, sealed with urethane, or some other hard-coat finish. These floors will always look polished and they never need waxing. They do not require as much effort to care for, but the finish is easily scratched by furniture. To clean them, boil 4 teabags in 1 quart of water and let it cool. The purpose of using tea as a scrubbing solution is to put color back into the floor. A few drops of mild dish soap in 1 gallon of warm water may be used also. Scrub one section at a time with a well-wrung-out rag and wipe dry to prevent water-spotting and warping.

The second type of floor has an oil or stain finish. It doesn't have a protective coating on it. I prefer this natural floor over the varnished floor because it will keep its beauty practically forever if it is well cared for. *Never put water (or any water-base floor-care products) on a natural hardwood floor!* Almost any kind of stain (milk spots, black scuff marks, crayon marks, tar, etc.) can be removed by dipping an SOS pad in paste floor wax and scrubbing.

If the floor really needs a good cleaning, use Bruce's Hardwood Floor Cleaner and Wax or Tre-wax Hardwood Floor Cleaner (see page 13). The wood-floor dealers also sell good cleaners and wax products. These are the only liquids I recommend for hardwood floors, and they should only be needed on rare occasions if the floor is swept and waxed regularly. After using the Bruce's or Tre-wax, a paste floor wax needs to be applied to give the floor protection and a high-gloss look.

For everyday care, dustmopping or sweeping with a fiber broom and then waxing are all that is needed. Wax helps a wood floor resist stains, spills, and wear. Wax two or three times a year for average-wear areas and three to six times a year for heavy-traffic areas. Consider the area under the throw rug a heavy-traffic area, because dirt and sand sift through the rug and get ground into the floor. New floors need to be waxed several times in the first six months. Always use a paste floor wax.

The secret to having a beautiful wood floor is to apply very thin coats of wax smoothly and evenly, following the grain or inlay of the wood. Let the wax dry for about twenty minutes, then buff with an electric buffer. The buffer smooths down the wax and gives the floor a more beautiful shine.

PAINTED
WOOD

Use 2 tablespoons of Murphy's Oil Soap or a few drops of mild dish soap in 1 gallon of warm water. Wash one section at a time with a well-wrung-out rag and wipe the section dry before moving on.

---

*The only place that success
comes before work is in the dictionary.*
—Arthur Brisbane

CONCRETE

Scrub with a heavy-duty cleaner like Spic and Span or Soilax. Use ¼ cup cleaner to 1 gallon hot water. Moderately dirty floors can be scrubbed with a mop. Really dirty floors should be scrubbed with a straw house broom, patio broom, or a scrub brush. Rinse to avoid a white, filmy look and wipe dry.

Tip: Fresh grease spills on a concrete driveway can be cleaned with kitty litter (from a pet-supply store). Sprinkle enough of the litter on the concrete to cover the stain. Rub it in with the ball of your shoe and then sweep it up.

To remove old grease, first soak it up with kitty litter, sand, or sawdust. Sweep it up and then pour enough Coke over the stain to cover it. This may take several cans. Let it soak for at least twenty minutes, but do not let it dry, then brush it out with a patio broom or scrub brush. This will leave a gray stain that can be whitened by scrubbing the concrete with a solution of 1 cup laundry detergent and 1 cup chlorine bleach in 1 gallon of hot water.

Prevent grease stains by cutting down a cardboard box and placing it under the leaky portion of the motor section whenever the car or other offender is standing in the driveway.

YOUR NOTES & CLEANING RECIPES

_____

_____

_____

_____

_____

_____

_____

_____

_____

_____

_____

_____

_____

_____

_____

_____

_____

_____

_____

_____

8 Furniture & Upholstery

Show me a home where the buffalo roam,
and I'll show you a messy house.

When you can see a child's well-outlined handprint on the coffee table, a good dusting is past due. The dust will scatter and float back on the furniture if you are not using a pretreated cloth. Dusting cloths are sold at very reasonable prices in most grocery stores. They can be used over and over again before they need to be washed, but after they are washed several times, the dust will not cling to them. A store-bought dustcloth can be restored by soaking it for eight hours in a few drops of liquid dish soap, a few drops of turpentine, and 1 quart of warm water. Wring out the cloth and hang it up to dry.

To make your own pretreated dustcloth, mix together 1 tablespoon mild soap powder (such as Ivory King, White Snow), 1 quart warm water, 1 tablespoon ammonia, and 2 tablespoons boiled linseed oil (found in paint and hardware stores; it is preboiled). Soak a good piece of flannel in the mixture for several minutes, then wring it out and hang it up to dry. Store the cloth in a covered glass or plastic container. Homemade dustcloths can be used for a long time before they have to be washed, but once they are washed, they have to be treated again.

WOODEN FURNITURE

Spray polish can be used on imitation-wood or plastic furniture finishes, but it should never be used on natural wood. When spray polish is used on veneer (a thin layer of beautiful, expensive wood glued to a cheaper surface), it may bubble, crack, or even lift the veneer off after several years. On more expensive wood pieces, spray polish can trap pollutants in the wood grain and actually damage the wood. A lot of furniture will become dirty, sticky, and dull-looking from spray-polish buildup. Sprays will turn walnut and mahogany a grayish color. I have heard antique dealers say that there will not be any antiques coming from our era because of the spray polishes that are used on the beautiful, expensive wood pieces.

Wood furniture is like a human skin. It needs oil to keep it beautiful. If wood becomes dried out it may split, warp, or crack. Oil will also help guard your beautiful wood furniture from permanent stains and discoloration. For light-colored furniture, such as oak and pecan, use Old English Scratch Cover for Light and Medium Wood, lemon oil, or Howard's Feed 'N Wax. For darker woods, such as walnut, use Old English Scratch Cover for Dark Wood. Old English Red oil is for cherry, mahogany, and other red-colored woods (page 11 and 12).

Dirt is not dirt,
but only matter in the wrong place.
—Lord Palmerston

You will need two old terry cloth rags, one to apply the oil and another to wipe it dry. When using light-colored oils, the rags can be washed in the washing machine, but *never* try to wash rags that are covered with dark oil. Use the same rag over and over again and store it in a shortening can between uses. Because furniture oil is flammable, *be careful not to store the rags by any kind of heat source.* After many uses, the rag used to apply the dark oil will get really gunky. Throw it away and use the wipe cloth to apply the oil and get a clean rag for wiping.

*Just about the time you think you can make ends meet,
someone comes along and moves the middle.*

WOOD CLEANING

Sometimes wood will need a good cleaning. Oil will not remove greasy fingerprints or other dirty marks. Also, if you change from sprays to oil, the wood furniture will become dull-looking, so the spray buildup should be removed first.

Mix together 2 tablespoons of linseed oil, 2 tablespoons turpentine, and 1 quart boiling water, as described earlier on page 56 (in the section on kitchen cabinets). Wearing disposable gloves (the smell will never come out of rubber gloves), dip a rag in the cleaner and wring it out until it is barely damp. Wash one area of the wood piece at a time, such as one side of an end table. Wipe it dry immediately, then go on to the next area of the furniture. Do not try to do a whole piece of furniture at once, because the water should never be allowed to soak on the wood. When the cleaner cools off, the oil and turpentine will separate from the water. Throw out the cleaner and make a completely new batch.

How often this treatment should be used depends on how rough the finish of the wood is and how many little greasy fingers you have around. Usually every three to six months is sufficient. Be sure to do it when the doors and windows can be opened, because it has a very strong odor.

---

*The man who brags "I run things in my home"
usually refers to the lawn mower,
the washing machine, the vacuum cleaner,
the baby carriage, and errands.*
—*Jacob M. Braude*

When I have explained this method for cleaning wood in the many talks that I give at clubs and churches, quite often someone will gasp, "You want me to use water on my beautiful wood furniture?" I have to laugh because usually this same person will not think twice about using spray polishes. This cleaner will not damage your furniture. The turpentine cleans it and the linseed oil puts the oil back into the wood. Very seldom do I have to put oil polish on the wood after I have used this cleaner, and the furniture looks beautiful. But for your peace of mind I will let you in on this secret: a lot of antique restorers and furniture refinishers use the same method. If you do not like this method, then use Murphy's Oil Soap. It is the second-best way to clean wood furniture.

The most popular labor-saving
device today is still a husband with money.
—Joey Adams

SPECIAL REMEDIES
Dull, Foggy, or Grayish-Hazed Wood. Use the wood cleaner described above. Another method is to mix together 1 tablespoon of vinegar and 1 quart of water. Using a cheesecloth, wash one small area at a time with the vinegar and water and wipe it dry. When the whole piece of furniture has been washed, polish it with oil.

Heat Marks. Heat marks can often be removed with spirits of camphor. Rub the camphor directly on the stain with a terrycloth rag and let it stand until it is dry. This usually takes about an hour. When it is dry, wipe it off with a clean rag. Then mix some lemon oil with rottenstone powder to make a paste. Rub it on the heat mark and polish the furniture with oil to bring back the luster. (Both spirits of camphor and rottenstone can be purchased at a hardware store.)

Paint. If the paint is fresh, wipe it away with a cloth soaked in furniture oil. If the paint has hardened, soak a cloth in linseed oil and put it on top of the paint. Let it stand until the paint has softened. This takes about two or three hours. Remove any paint traces with rottenstone and lemon oil mixed together to make a paste. Oil the furniture.

Water Rings. Rub Mentholatum, toothpaste, mayonnaise, or petroleum jelly into the white ring. Let it set for eight hours. Lightly sand with a dry Scotch Brite pad and polish with oil.

Light Surface Scratches. Take the meat out of a walnut and rub it into the scratch. The meat in the walnut will provide a filling and the oil will color it so the scratch is not as visible.

On dark furniture, Old English Scratch Cover will hide small scratches. Or fill in the scratch with a matching color of eyebrow pencil or permanent magic marker.

Middle age is when actions creak louder than words.

Deep Scratches. Buy a paste shoe polish that will match the color of your wood. Fill in the scratch with the paste. Rub over the scratch very lightly with a dry Scotch Brite pad, then polish.

Nature didn't make us perfect, so she
did the next best thing:
she made us blind to our faults.

---

98 **Tip:** Never put perfume or papers damp with duplicator fluid on any wood surface. This will leave a stain on the furniture that is impossible to remove. Always use coasters under glasses to prevent water rings.

Nothing makes you more tolerant
of a neighbor's noisy party than being there.
—Franklin P. Jones

PIANOS

Pianos are very complex instruments both inside and outside. On the inside, a piano has more moving parts than a car. On the outside, pianos are made out of many types of wood that have been treated and finished in different ways. The only universal advice that I can give about a piano is never to use spray polish on it. It is extremely difficult to repair or refinish the wood because the materials will not bond to surfaces with spray-polish buildup and the spray polish is almost impossible to remove completely.

The dealer who sold you the piano should be able to give you the best advice on how to care for it. If, for some reason, this source of information is unavailable to you, use the following guidelines:

1. Dust the piano often.

2. Clean smudges and fingerprints with a damp chamois (a soft, leatherlike cloth). Do one small section at a time and wipe it dry immediately.

3. Most pianos do not need to be polished with furniture oil. The oil will not penetrate the wood because of the hard, clear finish applied at the factory, and shiny spots will appear. On light wood, spotting is not too obvious, but on dark wood, especially ebony, it looks terrible. The oil will also make every fingerprint and smudge stand out.

4. Some pianos have a hand-rubbed, Danish oil finish. These pianos

should be polished occasionally with Danish oil, which can be purchased at a paint or hardware store. Apply it with a fine grade of steel wool or with very fine (wet or dry) sandpaper. Do one portion of the piano at a time, such as a leg or a side. Wipe the oil off and rub the wood dry with a soft cloth. If you don't know what kind of finish your piano has, consult a furniture refinisher.

5. Sometimes a piano will look dull and dirty. Spray-polish build-up, heavy smoking near the piano, dust and dirt accumulation, and/or lots of finger smudges will cause this. To clean the piano, use the wood-cleaning formula on page 56. Follow the instructions carefully. This will usually restore the beautiful shine.

Being right half the time
beats being half right all the time.
—Malcolm Forbes

Alcohol is a popular cleaner for piano keys, but it should never be used on real ivory keys. It will dry them out. The best cleaner is plain, unflavored yogurt. Rub it on and wipe it dry. White toothpaste applied with a damp cloth is also good. Buff it with a dry cloth. Be careful that the cleaner doesn't get between the keys. The yellowing of ivory keys is a desirable effect and adds to the beauty and value of the piano.

Murphy's law: No matter how long
or hard you shop for an item,
after you've bought it, it will be
on sale somewhere cheaper.

OTHER KINDS OF FURNITURE

CHROME AND GLASS

This is a great modern look that is not designed for old-fashioned kids. It is a showcase for every fingerprint and dirty smudge. If the chrome is really dirty and sticky, clean it with a solution of 2 tablespoons of Murphy's Oil Soap or a few drops of mild dish soap in 1 gallon of hot water. If it is only mildly dirty, clean it with 1 tablespoon of rubbing alcohol to 1 gallon of water. Wipe it dry to avoid water-spotting and streaking. To brighten the chrome, put rubbing alcohol on a rag and rub it on, then wipe it dry.

Keep a teaspoon of rubbing alcohol and a pint of water in a spray bottle for washing glass tabletops.

MARBLE TABLE TOPS

Treat the same as a marble floor (see page 90). A tabletop hopefully won't get the same heavy traffic as a floor, so it doesn't require waxing unless it becomes dull-looking.

WICKER AND RATTAN

Vacuum and dust frequently to prevent a dirty buildup. Wash with 2 teaspoons of Murphy's Oil Soap or a few drops of mild dish soap in 1 gallon of warm water. Scrub with a soaking-wet rag. Use a percolator brush or other narrow brush to get into hard-to-reach places. Wipe dry.

WROUGHT IRON

Clean the same as wicker and rattan. If the wrought iron is rusting, it is best to remove all traces of the rust with a rust removing agent like Naval Jelly and to sand and repaint.

UPHOLSTERY

Many of my clients have become my very close friends over the last thirty years. Several years ago I fell off a stepladder and broke my foot. Since I didn't have paid sick leave, I had to go back to work as soon as I could walk. Bless my friends, they were eager to have me back even with a cast slowing me down, and they tried very hard to make my work easy and light. Upholstery cleaning is often one of the simplest jobs in a house, but one of my good friends thought that it was too hard for me to handle with a broken foot. To save me the stress, she called in "professionals." Within hours her beautiful striped couch looked like something a junk-store dealer would refuse to sell. The colors had bled and run together. It looked sick and so did she.

Upholstery cleaners may not work on your furniture unless they have a signed statement releasing them from responsibility in case of shrinkage or other damage. So you take the same chance if you do it yourself—and you can bank the professional's big, fat fee.

A day of worry is more exhausting than a week of work.

WASHABLE UPHOLSTERY

Many of the new manmade fabrics like nylon, Dacron, polyester, Herculon, etc., are washable, but always check the label. If you have any doubts, test the upholstery on a small area that can't be seen, like the back of the chair or couch, and wait for a few hours. If the material doesn't streak or bleed, then go ahead and wash it. (Caution: Upholstery with dark colors, especially black, and upholstery that has been faded by the sun are very susceptible to bleeding.)

In one bucket mix together ½ cup of ammonia, ½ cup of cleaning solvent (page 12), and $\frac{1}{2}$ gallon of lukewarm water. If the upholstery is really dirty, add $\frac{1}{2}$ cup Spic and Span to this recipe. In a second bucket, add 1 cup vinegar to 1 gallon lukewarm water. Using an old towel, scrub the upholstery with the cleaning solvent and ammonia, then rinse it with another towel dipped in the vinegar and water. Use a third towel to wipe it as dry as possible.

If the couch or chair has removable cushion covers, take the covers off and wash them in the washing machine with warm water on a gentle cycle. Add $\frac{1}{4}$ cup vinegar to the rinse water. This will brighten the fabric. As soon as the washing machine stops, take the wet covers out, put them back on the cushions, and zip them up. The cushions will have to be patted back into shape, because they have a tendency to curl. Stand the cushions on their edges against the couch so that they can dry out thoroughly. Stains can be treated as if they were on your washable clothing (see Stain Removal Guide, pages 140–45).

---

*Entirely too many meetings open
at 7:30 sharp and end at 10:30 dull.*

UNWASHABLE UPHOLSTERY

Velvets, velveteens, and velours will spot, discolor, shrink, bleed and/or become stiff if water is placed on them. They must be cleaned with a cleaning solvent (page 12). Put the cleaning solvent on a terry cloth rag and scrub one section of the upholstery at a time with a circular motion. Then brush it back into its natural nap before moving on. Wipe it dry with a clean terry cloth rag. Test this method in a hard-to-see spot before doing the whole piece of furniture.

Rayons, cottons, tapestries, silks, and so on are very difficult to clean. They should only be cleaned by an *experienced* professional.

PREVENTIVE CARE

Vacuum the upholstery thoroughly at least twice a month. Keep the wrong side of the cushions turned up for daily wear, then, when you are expecting company, turn up the good side. The cushions will get double the wear and they will always look nice when they are needed.

I hate throw covers, because they look as if you are trying to hide something (and you usually are!). In the big, expensive homes I work in, the women use beautiful, decorative towels to protect their furniture. The bath size can be used on a couch and the hand size is used on chair seats, backs, and armrests (especially upholstered dining-room chairs). Towels are a necessity because dark clothes destroy the beauty of upholstery. Jeans are really hard on any kind of velvet or light upholstery. They leave a dark stain wherever they have been. Hair grease is difficult to remove from chair backs or any other place the head rests. You will be surprised how dirty those towels will get. When company comes, the towels can be removed very quickly and thrown in the closet.

MORE TIPS

If the cushions are getting worn out in the front, blindstitch the flaps over the zipper so that the zipper can't be seen, then turn the cushions around so that the zipper is in the front.

On threadbare spots where white shows through on the cushion or the cording, color it with a permanent Magic Marker that matches the color of the upholstery.

The wise woman will always
let her husband have her way.
—Richard Brinsley Sheridan

SLIPCOVERS

Wash slipcovers in the washing machine on a gentle cycle. Remove from the machine and iron only the flounces. While the material is still wet, put the slipcover back on the chair or couch. This not only eliminates the hard work of ironing, but it produces a better fit.

VINYL UPHOLSTERY

Most vinyl upholstery is washable. Use 3 tablespoons of Murphy's Oil Soap to $^1/_2$ gallon of hot water and wipe dry. Really dirty upholstery may need to be cleaned with turpentine. *Do not use turpentine near an open flame or furnace vent.* Put it on an old rag and scrub the vinyl, then wash the turpentine off with Murphy's Oil Soap and hot water.

LEATHER

Leather upholstery is very durable and will last a long time if it is well cared for. Vacuum and dust it often. It should never have much water on it, but for emergency cleaning, use a few drops of mild dish soap in a gallon of warm water. Scrub it with a slightly dampened cloth.

For deep cleaning use saddle soap. Leather, like wood, needs to be oiled occasionally or it may dry out, become brittle and crack. Saddle soap contains lanolin derived from sheep's wool, so it puts oil back into the leather. If you are not using saddle soap then occasionally recondition the leather by applying a layer of castor oil or cod liver oil to the surface. Rub it in with your fingers, let it soak into the leather for at least an hour and then wipe it dry.

Whilest Adam slept, Eve from his side arose:
Strange his first sleep would be his last repose.

YOUR NOTES & CLEANING RECIPES

9 Windows & Other Glass

A smile is a light in the window of the soul,
indicating that the heart is at home.

Windows are very important to the total "clean" look of a home. If the windows are dirty, the house loses that crisp, sparkling appearance. How easy it would be to keep all the windows clean if it weren't for smog, sudden rainstorms on the one day in the month you decided to wash them, or, even worse, thundershowers of kids pouring in with tiny smudgy hands that seem to be magnetically pulled to that beautiful, big, clean picture window as it sparkles in the sun.

Still, there is a way to fool most of the people, most of the time. Just make sure that the front storm-door window and front picture window are always clean. Most people never see beyond these two points anyway. It takes a few extra minutes, but it is well worth the sparkle that it adds to the entrance hall or front room. You will be surprised how often other women, especially young mothers, are awed by a clean, glistening front window.

How busy is not so important as why busy.
The bee is praised; the mosquito is swatted.

WINDOWS

BASIC CLEANER

I don't like to use commercial window cleaners. They are too expensive for the job when cheap rubbing alcohol and water will clean as well or better than most brands. Use 2 tablespoons of rubbing alcohol to 2 quarts of *hot* water (cold water will never clean as well as hot water). This will make the windows glisten and you won't have to spend time getting out streaks as you do with some commercial window cleaners or ammonia.

In cold weather, use 2 tablespoons of cornstarch to 1 quart of warm water.

Experience is a hard teacher—
she gives the test first, the lesson afterwards.

PROBLEMS

Hard-Water Stains. Hard water forms a white deposit on the windows that is really hard to get off. If the windows are only mildly stained, pour undiluted white vinegar on a rag and scrub. For worse problems, use Lysol Toilet Bowl Cleaner. (Caution: Do not use Lysol on a hot, sunny window because it will smoke up, dry immediately, and leave a hard-to-remove white film on the window.) Squirt it directly from the bottle onto the window and scrub, then clean the window with the basic cleaner. Be sure to use rubber gloves.

Hard-to-Reach Windows. Fuller Brush sells a squeegee and brush extension that will reach second-story windows. Dip the brush in the window cleaner and scrub, then wipe down the window with the squeegee. So that the window won't streak, secure a big wad of rag on the squeegee with pins or elastic bands and dry the window.

Impossible-to-Reach Windows. This method takes off the dirt but leaves some streaks. Put 2 to 3 tablespoons dishwasher soap and 1 tablespoon Jet Dry (found next to the dishwasher soaps in many grocery stores) in a spray-bottle hose attachment that is used to spray insecticides. Fill the spray bottle with water, attach it to the hose, and spray one section of window at a time. Rinse that section immediately with clean water. The water will sheet off, so there is no need to dry the window.

WIPING MATERIALS

Newspaper. Wiping materials are as important as the window cleaner. Scrunched-up newspaper is best, but it makes your hands black.

Percale or Cotton Rags. The next-best thing is old percale or cotton rags. Percale is a type of cotton material that was used a lot for making sheets before permanent press was invented. (Those were also the days when sheets didn't have magic fitted corners.) Check with your mother or grandmother to see if they might have some percale rags stored away.

Never use permanent press for any kind of cleaning. Because of the finish it is not absorbent, so it just smears and streaks the water all over the windows.

Paper Towels. Most paper towels can't stand the torment of washing windows. They either fall apart or they glide over the water and the window like the permanent press. Bounty and Brawny are the best brand names I have found for window washing. Old napkins also make great lint-free *polishing* cloths for windows and mirrors.

Squeegees. I hate to use them for washing windows, because they leave long streaks. On hard-to-reach windows, they are almost a necessity, but avoid using them on windows that are readily seen by visitors.

Squeegees can be rejuvenated by placing them on a flat surface and gently rubbing them with fine sandpaper.

WASHING TIPS

Streaks. Wash the windows from left to right on the inside and from top to bottom on the outside. Then if they streak, you know which side the streak is on. Early morning is the best time to wash windows, because the streaks can be seen better then. Never wash windows in the hot sun because they dry too fast and leave streaks.

Fog-Free Windows. Wipe the windows with a rag dipped in glycerine (this can be purchased at a pharmacy).

Frost-Free Windows. Wash the windows with undiluted rubbing alcohol.

Aluminum Window Frames. Scrub with an SOS pad, then put a few drops of household oil on the tracks. This helps them to stay cleaner and glide more easily.

SCREENS

If the screens are removable, line them up against an outside wall or fence and rinse them off with the hose. The force of the water will remove most of the dirt. If the screens have greasy dirt or if they are not removable, then use 2 tablespoons of Spic and Span or Soilax in 1 gallon of hot water. Scrub with a nylon brush and blot dry with a terrycloth rag.

The only thing you get without working is hungry.

OTHER GLASS CATEGORIES

Mirrors. I like to keep a teaspoon of rubbing alcohol and a pint of water in a spray bottle for washing mirrors and spot-cleaning windows.

Gilded mirror frames can be wiped clean with beer. Pour it on a soft rag, rub gently, and wipe dry.

Speech is a mirror of the soul:
as a man speaks, so he is.
—Publilius Syrus

CHANDELIERS

If this method is used often the chandelier will really sparkle without all the drudgery and work of taking apart the prisms. Be sure the lights are off and cool. Place a big towel under the chandelier. Put 2 teaspoons of rubbing alcohol and 1 pint of *warm* water in a spray bottle and drench the chandelier. Let it drip dry. The alcohol water will not hurt brass, stainless steel, copper, or gold light fixtures.

Some chandeliers may be too dirty for this method to work the first time. If this is the case, then take down the prisms and wash them in a plastic bucket with *hot* water and 2 tablespoons of rubbing alcohol.

LIGHT FIXTURES

Hurricanes, chimneys, smokey and clear-glass globes, and other glass light covers should be washed at least once a month. The lighting isn't as bright when it has to filter through a dusty cover and it makes the whole room look dingy. They should be washed in a plastic bucket to avoid breakage and chipping. Use 2 tablespoons rubbing alcohol to 2 quarts hot water.

Hard work is an accumulation of
easy things you didn't do when you should have.

CRYSTAL

Stubborn stains on crystal can be removed easily with a cloth dipped in turpentine.

EYEGLASSES

When cleaning eyeglasses, a drop of vinegar or rubbing alcohol will really make them shiny and clear.

GLASS VASES

Rinse out the vase with warm water. Pour in enough cold tea or vinegar to cover the stains and let it soak for eight hours. If the stain is still there, then squirt it with Lysol Toilet Bowl Cleaner. Make sure to put the vase in a high locked cupboard, away from the reach of children. Let it set for eight hours, then pour the Lysol in the toilet and wash out the vase.

A good laugh is sunshine in a house.
—William M. Thackeray

TIPS:

Remove tiny scratches from glass by rubbing them with toothpaste. Pick up small pieces of broken glass with a damp paper towel.

YOUR NOTES & CLEANING RECIPES

10 Drapes & Other Window Dressings

DRAPES

I recommend that you take your drapes to the cleaners about once every fifteen years. Surprised? One reason is that they are very costly to dry-clean, but the most important reason is that they lose their beauty after being dry-cleaned; sometimes they will even shrink.

Drapes can have a long, beautiful life if they are well cared for. Vacuum-clean them thoroughly at least once a month. Do the inside of the drapes first. Using the upholstery brush, start at the top of the panel and work down. When the inside is vacuumed, then do the outside in the same way.

Beauty is skin deep,
but ugly goes all the way to bone.

About every six months, take down the drapes, tape down the hooks with masking tape, and run them through a **NO-HEAT** cycle (fifteen minutes) in the dryer with a damp towel. The dust will cling to the towel. *Take the drapes out as soon as the dryer stops.* If you let them sit in the dryer, they will get wrinkled. Peel off the tape and rehang immediately!

If the draperies are identical twins, then switch them. Put the drape that was on the right side on the left, and hang the drape that was on the left side on the right. To find out if this is possible, you have to examine the side hems. The hem in the middle opening must have the same number of inches from the edge to the first pleat as the other hem that goes around the curtain rod. Switching the draperies will add years to their life. This will move those precious little finger marks that are now in the middle around to the back where no one can see them. It will also distribute the sun rot more evenly. If the drapes are hung in south or west windows, dry cleaners will not guarantee them because of the strong sun that comes through those windows. When purchasing drapes for your south or west windows, be sure to get ones that can be switched.

A baby is an angel whose
wings decrease as his legs increase.
—French proverb

SHEERS

Sheers made from washable materials like Dacron, nylon, and Herculon should never be sent to the dry cleaners. These manmade fabrics are washable, and dry-cleaning will turn them gray or dark. Sometimes it puts wrinkles in that can't be removed. If you are not sure the sheers are washable, then take them to a cleaners and ask. If the cleaners are reputable, they will tell you if the sheers should be washed or dry-cleaned.

There are two methods to use in washing sheers:

1. **BATHTUB.** Put the sheers in the bathtub in really warm water to which 2 tablespoons of liquid detergent (Wisk, Dynamo, Era, etc.) has been added. Swish them around every ten minutes for about an hour. Let the water drain out. Fill the bathtub again with warm water **115**

and add ¼ cup of vinegar. The vinegar helps to break down the soap and it also brightens the sheers. Swish the sheers around and then empty the water. Rinse them one more time in the same way. Put the hooks back into the sheers while they are still in the rinse water. Place several layers of towels on the floor under the window and then hang up the sheers soaking wet. *Do not wring them out.* Reshape the sheers while they are drying by starting at the top and pulling down on each fold of pleat. Continue to do this until they are dry. It takes about twenty minutes. The top stiffening material (buckram) and the hem will take about an hour to dry. (If the buckram is more than ten years old it may not be washable.) Reshape the pleats in the buckram by putting a spring clothespin on each one, or just keep pinching the pleats together with your fingers.

*About the only thing we have left
that actually discriminates in favor o' the
plain people is the stork.*
—Frank McKinney Hubbard

2. **WASHING MACHINE.** Put the sheers in the washing machine on a gentle cycle in warm water. (Cold water will not work. The warm water breaks down the dirt and grime.) Use any good detergent. Add ¼ cup of vinegar to the rinse cycle. The whole secret in washing sheers in the washer is to *never let them spin out.* This causes wrinkles. Take the sheers out of the washer after the rinse cycle and let the water spin out. Reset the dial to the rinse cycle. When the washer is full of water, add ¼ cup of vinegar and put the sheers in. At the end of the second rinse, stop the machine again. Put the hooks back into the sheers while they are still in the washer. Put bath towels under the windows and hang the sheers up

soaking wet. Reshape the sheers in the same way as the bathtub method, described above.

Your sheers will have very few wrinkles with these methods and it will only cost very little per window to wash them.

OTHER WINDOW COVERINGS

LOUVER DOORS

Wash with 2 tablespoons Murphy's Oil Soap in 1 gallon hot water. Wrap a small rag around a butter knife or purchase a narrow painting sponge (the type used for tight corners) to clean each slat quickly.

LEVOLOR BLINDS

For monthly cleaning use a pre-treated dust cloth, like One-Wipe (page 16). These work especially well on dark blinds which are difficult to wash, because even the best rags leave small specks of lint and streak marks. Light-colored blinds may need a good washing. For this a cotton garden glove is handy (pun intended). Use 3 tablespoons of Murphy's Oil Soap in 2 quarts of hot water. Dip the garden glove in the solution, wring out slightly and put it on. Place your fingers between the slats and slide them across the blind. You can do four slats at a time with this method and usually you don't have to wipe the blinds dry.

Bachelors are providential beings;
God created them for the
consolation of widows and the hope of maids.
—J. De Finod

VENETIAN BLINDS

Slip an old stocking or cotton glove on your hand to dust venetian blinds. Occasionally they will need a good scrubbing, especially if they are in the kitchen or bathroom where they will collect a lot of greasy dirt. Fill the bathtub half-full with hot water and add 2 tablespoons of liquid dish soap. Take down the blinds and soak them in the tub for a few minutes, then wash, rinse, and wipe them dry. Put a washrag over a butter knife to get at the hard-to-reach corners.

VINYL SHADES

These are usually very dirty so strong soapsuds should be used to clean them. Use ¼ cup Spic and Span or Soilax in 1 gallon of hot water. Spread the shade on a large table, the floor, or on a clean sidewalk. Scrub with a terrycloth rag and wipe dry.

BAMBOO SHADES

Use 2 tablespoons Murphy's Oil Soap or a few drops of a mild liquid dish soap in 1 gallon hot water. Scrub both sides with a terrycloth rag and wipe it dry. If the shade can be removed from the window, stretch it out on the floor or table or take it outside on the sidewalk or driveway to scrub it. If it can not be removed, fold a large bath towel so that it is a little larger than your hand, then hold it directly opposite and on the other side of the portion of the shade which is being scrubbed. This supports the bamboo and keeps it from bending or breaking.

UNWASHABLE SHADES

These should be vacuumed at least once a month to keep the dirt from building up. When it is necessary to clean them, use a wallpaper cleaner (sold at a hardware or paint store).

YOUR NOTES & CLEANING RECIPES

_____

_____

_____

_____

_____

_____

_____

_____

_____

_____

_____

_____

_____

_____

_____

_____

_____

_____

11 Walls & Woodwork

Sometimes you get discouraged
Because I am so small,
And always leave my fingerprints
On furniture and wall.

But every day I'm growing up
And soon I'll be so tall,
That all those little handprints
Will be hard to recall.
—Unknown

Flat paint is one of the housekeeper's worst enemies. Contractors use it a lot in new homes because it is cheaper than the glossy paints. Dirt sticks to flat paint and walls won't come clean when washed. Always paint with a satin, semigloss, or glossy paint.

Dirt also adheres to textured walls. Wherever a scrub rag has been, it will leave a track unless the area is immediately wiped. Only rags with a very tight weave can be used on a textured wall, because the wall will pick up the lint and threads from a loosely woven fabric, like terry cloth. It is easier to repaint a textured wall than to scrub it. Even after it is scrubbed it doesn't look really clean.

Ceilings have the same problem. It is almost impossible to scrub a ceiling so that it looks clean and beautiful, because the dirt is usually greasy. When women ask me about washing ceilings, I always tell them that if it looks bad enough to wash, then it is time to repaint. The results will be much more pleasing (especially if you can get someone else to do all the hard work).

WASHABLE WALLS

For quick pickup of smudges and fingerprints on all washable wall surfaces, keep on hand in a spray bottle some of the following formula (I also use this for exterior surfaces on large kitchen appliances): 2 tablespoons nonsudsy ammonia, 1 teaspoon liquid dish soap, 1 pint rubbing alcohol, and 1 gallon water. It is as effective as the magic wall cleaners that can be purchased in the store. Just spray it on, then wipe it off. The dirt almost melts away (but your money stays around to play).

MILD DIRT

I use Murphy's Oil Soap on washable wall surfaces (except those coated with flat paint), including paneling, if the wall is only *mildly* dirty. *Do not use Murphy's Oil Soap if you are preparing to paint!* The paint will not adhere to the oil. Before painting use one of the cleaners described below under Heavy Dirt. Begin at the top of the wall and wash down. To prevent streaking, always wipe it dry. If you don't like ladders and a stiff neck, then use a long-handled sponge mop. After washing the wall, throw a clean towel over the mop and wipe it dry.

Put a smile on your kisser and maybe someone will put a kiss on your smiler!

HEAVY DIRT

If the walls are really dirty and greasy or if they are finished with flat paint, then use ¼ cup of Spic and Span or Soilax to 1 gallon of hot water, **121** or make your own wall cleaner. In 1 gallon of hot water, mix 1 cup ammonia, ½ cup white vinegar, and ¼ cup baking soda. Wash the wall, starting with the bottom first to avoid making dirty water streaks that will not come out. The water will not mark the clean area below if it is changed often and kept clean. Use a terrycloth rag to scrub and wipe the wall dry with a clean rag. (Note: This cleaner is so strong it may dull a glossy wall.)

STAINS

A friend of my daughter-in-law kept finding creative crayon artwork on her walls and floors. With several small children, anyone could have done it, but no one would ever admit to it. One day as she noticed a particularly masterful piece on the hall wall in bright reds and greens, she called all of her children to her.

"Which one of you drew this beautiful picture?" she asked, full of admiration.

The four-year-old artist quickly identified his work. That day he learned one of the great truths of our age: some of our most talented artists are never appreciated while they are alive.

Discipline is what you inflict
on one end to impress the other.

Crayon. Put turpentine on a rag and wipe off the crayon, or rub toothpaste on the crayon mark and then scrub with a damp rag. Some crayons have a dye that is almost impossible to remove without an SOS pad. It will take off some of the finish on the wall, but that's better than a crayon mark.

Ball-Point Ink. Spray the pen mark with cheap hairspray and wipe it off. Another method is to mix together 1 tablespoon of fresh lemon juice

and ½ teaspoon of salt. Put this on with a damp rag and wipe it off.
Scotch Tape. Remove tape from walls without damaging the paint by pressing it with a warm iron first.

A vacation consists of:
2 weeks,
which are 2 short,
after which you are 2 tired
2 return
2 work
and 2 broke
not 2!

WALLPAPER

CLEANING

Walltex or vinyl-coated wallpapers are beautiful to keep up. Wash them with Lin-Sol, or make your own cleaner by mixing together ¼ cup ammonia, a few drops of liquid dish soap, and 1 gallon warm water. Stains in walltex or vinyl-coated wallpaper can be removed by using the same methods described for walls.

Some wallpapers cannot be washed. These should be dusted quite often so dirt doesn't built up. Use a vacuum cleaner or dust mop, or throw a towel over a broom and go over each wall. In fact, if you did this to all your walls they wouldn't have to be washed very often because the dirt wouldn't accumulate.

Wallpaper cleaner is sold in hardware stores. Powdered borax can also be used on slightly soiled wallpaper. Rub it on with a clean cloth and then wipe it off.

STAINS (WASHABLE OR UNWASHABLE WALLPAPER)

Most stains can be removed with the wallpaper cleaner. An art-gum

123

eraser will also remove stains. If the wallpaper is really soiled, it may look worse after a stain is removed, because it will leave a clean spot that will make the rest of the wallpaper look filthy.

Crayon. Scrape off as much of the crayon as possible with a knife. Make a paste by mixing a cleaning solvent (see page 12) and powdered whiting (sold at a paint store). Apply this paste thickly over the crayon. When it is dry, brush off the powder. Repeat if necessary.

Ink. Blot up as much as possible with paper towels or an ink blotter. Apply cornstarch and brush it off.

Grease. A simple method is to make a paste out of cornstarch and cleaning solvent. Rub it on the wallpaper and let it stand for two days. At the end of the second day, brush if off. Fresh grease will always leave a ring or a stain, but a lot of it can be removed this way.

Another method is to put an ink blotter over the spot and press it with a warm iron several times. Be careful not to scorch the wallpaper. Then, make a paste out of fuller's earth and cleaning solvent (both of these can be purchased at a hardware store). Rub the paste on the grease, let it dry thoroughly, and wipe it off.

People who think they know everything
are particularly aggravating to those of us who do.

FOIL

If the foil is unwashable follow the directions for unwashable wallpaper. Some washable foils are not very scrub-resistant. The pattern may be damaged easily or wiped completely off, so be very careful. Clean it with a damp rag and wipe it dry.

On unflocked washable foils, lemon oil can be used for cleaning. Put the oil on a rag and wash the wall, then wipe it dry. This will leave a beautiful shine.

PANELING

Do not use spray polish on any kind of paneling. It will streak and collect the dust so that the paneling gets dirty fast. On natural wood paneling use the wood-cleaning formula given in Chapter 5 (page 56) or Murphy's Oil Soap in hot water. Be sure to wipe it dry so the wood won't warp and the plastic finishes won't go dull and have water spots.

For light-colored *real wood* paneling, such as oak and pecan, use Old English Scratch Cover for Light and Medium Wood, lemon oil, Johnson's Jubilee Cleaner, or Howard's Feed 'N Wax. For darker wood paneling, such as walnut, use Old English Scratch Cover for Dark Wood. Old English Red oil is for cherry, mahogany, and other red-colored woods (page 11 and 12). Rub the polish dry with a clean rag or the dirt and dust will stick to it.

To cover scratches on plastic paneling, use a liquid shoe polish or an eyebrow pencil that is the same color as the finish.

A rich man is nothing but a poor man with money.
—W. C. Fields

TILE

Tile walls are cleaned differently from tile showers and tile kitchen counters. Use 2 tablespoons of Spic and Span or Soilax in 1 gallon of hot water. Scrub with a terrycloth rag or a nylon scrub brush, then wipe it dry. If the tile needs a shine, put lemon oil on a rag and rub the wall surface, then wipe dry. To whiten the tile and get rid of mildew, add a tablespoon of liquid bleach to the wash water.

YOUR NOTES & CLEANING RECIPES

_____

_____

_____

_____

_____

_____

_____

_____

_____

_____

_____

_____

_____

_____

_____

_____

_____

_____

12 Laundry & Stain Removal

If the father of our country, George Washington,
was Tutankhamened tomorrow, and, after being
aroused from his tomb, was told that the American people
today spend two billion dollars yearly
on bathing (and washing) material,
he would say, "What got 'em so dirty?"
—*Will Rogers*

We think that it is wonderful to live in a time when modern conveniences do all the hard work. Actually, I sometimes wonder if life wasn't a bit easier in the olden days when there weren't any washing machines. The old homes were built with hooks instead of closets, because people back then only had two changes of clothes: one to work in and one to go to church in. (Think of it, no closets to clean!) You didn't have to wash the work clothes until they could stand up and crawl in the water by themselves, and you were not allowed to get the church clothes dirty. Underwear was seldom washed. Even the great royalty, with all their beautiful gowns, wore only one pair of underwear during the winter. It is reported that Queen Elizabeth I of England was sewn into her underwear in the fall and cut out of it in the spring. The smell didn't bother them. It would be like eating garlic: if everyone smells, then no one minds.

Can you imagine it? Those people didn't have to sit through commercials and watch someone rave about her bleach and fabric softener. **127**

There were no big decisions to make about whether to buy the white detergent with the blue spots or the blue detergent that guarantees it will make everything look whiter. It wasn't until washing became so convenient that cleanliness came into style. We have paid dearly in water, soap, extra clothes, and time for the invention of that great labor-saver, the washer.

I'm as old as my tongue,
and a little older than my teeth.
—Jonathan Swift

LOOK FOR THE LABEL

When purchasing new clothes or fabrics, always pay special attention to the washing instructions on the label. This is the easiest and safest way to determine how a garment should be cared for. Labels will also state what can damage the fabric; for example, *Do not dry-clean, No bleach, Do not wring,* etc.

Be aware of labels indicating that a garment will take extra time for individual care or extra money for professional care. Some labels that indicate special attention are:

WASHING

No spin — Remove article from washing machine before the final spin cycle.

Wash separately — Wash alone or with other articles that are the same color.

Hand-wash — Wash by hand. Usually this indicates that the temperature of the water should be cool to lukewarm.

DRYING

Drip dry

Remove from washing machine *before* final spin and hang wet. Do not dry in a dryer.

Line dry

Remove from washing machine after the final spin. Hang damp. Do not dry in a dryer.

Dry flat

Lay garment on bath towels on a flat surface to dry.

The following labels indicate extra expense:

SPECIAL CLEANING

Dry-clean only

Garment can be dry-cleaned either by a professional cleaners or at a self-service laundry.

Professionally dry-clean only

Self-service dry-cleaning cannot be used.

Flame-resistant garments are also labeled and the instructions need to be followed or the garment will lose its flame-resistant quality. Usually these specially treated fabrics need to be washed with a detergent containing phosphates (see page 132).

There are two days about which nobody should worry,
and these are yesterday and tomorrow.
—Robert Jones Burdette

BEFORE YOU WASH

1. Empty every pocket. Pens, crayons, coins, sharp objects, etc., might damage the washing machine and/or damage or stain the fabrics.

Facial tissue and other paper products spread obnoxious lint all over everything.

2. Fasten all hooks, including those on bras. Close zippers and tie long strings, such as apron strings, to prevent snagging and tangling.

3. Turn corduroy, permanent-press, and knit garments inside out.

4. Always remove stains before washing (see Stain Removal Guide, pages 140–45). Pay special attention to collars and cuffs and pretreat them with a prewash stain remover (page 138) if they are dirty or oily.

LAUNDRY SORTING CHART

TEMPERATURE	Normal-Regular Cycle
Hot-Water Wash *Warm-Water Rinse	Heavily soiled work and play clothes, white and colorfast cottons, white linens, diapers, tennis shoes, white socks, light-colored corduroys, heavily soiled elastic garments, mattress pads
Warm-Water Wash *Warm-Water Rinse	Moderately soiled work and play clothes, colored cottons and linens, moderately soiled elastic garments, washable blankets, throw rugs, plastics (raincoats, baby panties), dark and colored corduroys
Cold-Water Wash *Cold-Water Rinse	Sturdy or regular noncolorfast cottons, linens, and corduroys; other fabrics that bleed

SORTING THE LAUNDRY

It amazes me how many women put their jeans in the washing machine with their white clothes and then wonder why they all come out with a blue tint. For best results, clothing should be separated according to the cycle (normal, permanent press, delicate) and the temperature (hot, warm, cold). Study the Laundry Sorting Chart below. In addition, the following fabrics should be sorted and washed separately:

1. Fabrics that give out lint such as bath towels or terrycloth rags.
2. White clothes.
3. Colorfast fabrics: these should be separated from noncolorfast fabrics, then separated again into light and dark colors.
4. Heavily soiled clothes.

Permanent Press Cycle

Sturdy, heavily soiled permanent-press work and play clothes, white nylon, white polyester, and white double-knit fabrics. (These should be rinsed in cold water.)

Sturdy and regular moderately soiled permanent-press work and play clothes (cold-water rinse), colored socks, man-made colorfast fabrics (acrylic, polyester, nylon. etc.). (Rinse in cold water.)

Delicate, slightly soiled permanent-press

Gentle-Delicate Cycle

Delicate white fabrics, delicate, heavily soiled permanent-press (cold-water rinse), light-colored, washable bedspreads, quilts, and quilted bathrobes

Delicate colored fabrics, hosiery, washable woolens, medium- and dark-colored washable bedspreads, quilts, and quilted bathrobes, man-made fiber knits (acrylic, polyester, nylon, etc.). (Rinse in cold water.)

Delicate noncolorfast fabrics that bleed

*Unless otherwise specified

131

WASHING TIPS

LAUNDRY DETERGENTS

With all the bright boxes lined up on the store shelves, it is difficult to choose the best laundry detergent for your wash. A detergent that your neighbor claims is fantastic may make your laundry look gray and dingy. It is obvious that all detergents are not alike. There are actually three different types:

1. **PHOSPHATE DETERGENTS** (Bold, Tide, Cheer, Cold Power, All, Dash, etc.). All detergents must list their phosphorus content. It is usually located on the side of the box at the bottom. Some communities have banned the sale of detergents with phosphates because they promote the growth of algae which chokes up rivers, lakes, and streams.

Detergents containing phosphate wash well in all temperatures and are excellent for use in all levels of hard and soft water.

2. **NONPHOSPHATE DETERGENTS** (Purex, Sun, White King, etc.). These detergents perform well in soft water, but nonphosphate detergents should generally *not* be used in hard-water area unless your home is equipped with a water softener. If a nonphosphate detergent is used in hard water, garments may become gray, discolored, and/or harsh to the touch. This happens because the nonphosphate detergent does not break down all the hard-water curds and they cling to the fabric. Another side effect is that hard-water residue will build up on the interior washer parts and eventually cause them to malfunction.

Using hot water and water softeners (Calgon, Blue Rain Drops, White King Water Softener, etc.) with a nonphosphate detergent will minimize the hard-water problems. Pouring the detergent in the water and letting it agitate for several minutes before adding the clothes will also help to soften the water. *Note:* The local water department can tell you the degree of hardness in your water.

3. SOAPS   (Ivory King, White Snow, etc.). Many people prefer to use these very mild soaps rather than detergents for laundering. Soap works well in soft water, but it reacts the same way a nonphosphate detergent does in hard water.

Tips: Always measure the detergent. Don't just dump! Use the recommended amount for a guideline, but remember that more detergent (as much as fifty percent more) may need to be added to the wash if the water is hard, the load is large or heavily soiled, and/or if you are using stain-removal procedures.

Detergent should be added to the water *before* the clothes are put in. Do not put the detergent on top of the clothing.

BLEACHES

Bleach will whiten and brighten clothes. It can help remedy dingy and gray clothes and it is important when removing stains.

CHLORINE BLEACHES   (Clorox, Purex, Western Shores, etc.). These should never be used on silk, acetates, wool, or elastic (Spandex) fabrics. It may also make some fabrics which have been treated with resin, turn yellow. If you are uncertain whether a garment can be bleached, perform this simple test. Dilute 1 teaspoon of bleach in 3 tablespoons of water. Place a few drops of diluted bleach on an inconspicuous area, like the inside of the hem or an inside seam. Let it stand for five minutes, then blot it dry. If the fabric doesn't discolor or bleed, then it can be safely bleached. If the washing-instruction label states "no chlorine bleach," then do not use liquid or powdered bleaches that contain chlorine.

When using a chlorine bleach, follow the directions on the bottle and measure accurately. Do not use more than 1 cup of bleach in a load of wash. Fill the washer with water and add the bleach. Allow the washer to agitate before adding the clothes. Or, after the water and clothes are in the washer and the washer is agitating, bleach can be added by diluting it

133

with 1 quart of water. Pouring undiluted bleach on the fabrics will cause damage.

OXYGEN BLEACHES (LaFrance, Snowy, Clorox 2, etc.). These can be used even if the clothes label reads "no chlorine bleach." They are usually safe for all washable fabrics, but do not use them if the label reads "no bleach." For the best results, fill the washer with water, add the detergent, and then the clothes. Let the washer agitate several minutes before the oxygen bleach is added to allow the brighteners in the detergent time to do their work. Oxygen bleach cleans best in hot water.

Wrinkles should merely indicate where smiles have been.
—Mark Twain

FABRIC SOFTENERS

Repairmen and salespeople love fabric softeners, because they shorten the life of the washing machine and dryer. A harmless, cheap way to get rid of static cling and soften the clothes is to add ⅛ cup of white vinegar to the rinse water. This also breaks down the soap residue so that the clothes, especially the dark clothes, look brighter. There is a slight vinegar smell while the clothes are still wet but it goes away as soon as they dry. Hairspray can also be used to remove static cling (see page 139).

COMMON MISTAKES

Overloading the Washing Machine. This causes wrinkling, especially in permanent-press clothes. It also causes browning or yellowing when clothes are ironed because the detergent hasn't been rinsed out properly. And finally, it results in dingy, gray clothes because there are too many clothes and too little water for the detergent to clean adequately.

Follow the manufacturer's guidelines for suggested loads. Clothes should not be packed down. They should be placed in the washing machine lightly so that they can move freely. Permanent-press clothes should be loaded lighter than other clothes. When possible, wash small and large items together.

Wrong Temperature. It is important to use hot water (140°F.) when it is recommended. Dingyness, graying, or yellowing can be caused if the water is not hot enough to break down dirt, body oils, and hard-water curds. If several washes are being done, conserve the hot water for the wash cycle by rinsing with cold water. Also, allow time for water to heat up between washes by alternating hot, warm, and cold washes.

Check the Laundry Sorting Chart on pages 130–31 for recommended wash temperatures.

DRYING

Remove clothes as soon as the dryer has stopped to prevent wrinkling. It is easy to get busy and forget that the clothes are drying if there is not a buzzer to indicate when the machine has stopped. To remedy this problem, buy a manual timer or set the timer on your stove to ring when the clothes should come out.

Do not overdry clothes. This causes wrinkling, buildup of static electricity, and shrinkage. Permanent-press clothes need to be taken out while they are slightly damp. If the dryer stops and some clothes are damp but others are dry, remove the dry clothes before starting the machine again.

Do not dry too many clothes at a time. They must have room to fluff. Pillows, mattress pads, curtains, throw rugs, and coats can be fluffed up by putting them in the dryer on a no-heat cycle. This will also take out lint, dust, and dog hairs.

Solar Drying. The smell of clothes dried out in the fresh air is great (provided you don't live in a high-pollution area). I especially like to hang my blankets and sheets outside to dry. Permanent-press items come out better if they are dried in a dryer.

Blankets and clothes made out of corduroy may need the nap brushed up if they are line-dried.

What, sir, would the people of
the earth be without woman? They would be scarce, sir, almighty scarce.
—Mark Twain

Finishing Tips: Fold tablecloths with the wrong side out so if the crease becomes soiled or discolored it won't show on the table. To prevent most creases, hang the tablecloth on a wooden hanger in the closet.

If your linens are yellow, add bleach to the wash and then spread the linens out in the hot sun on the grass. This will take out the yellow.

Every cloud has its silver lining,
but it is sometimes a little difficult to get it to the mint.
—Don Marquis

To remove water spots from silk, let it dry, then rub it briskly with another part of the silk.

Iron ribbons by pulling the ribbon rather than pushing the iron.

When ironing lace, dip it first in a solution of 2 teaspoons of sugar and 1 pint of water. It will not scorch.

Lightly starch pillowcases to prevent staining by hair oils or creams.

Pin stockings together to save a lot of time trying to mate them. Better yet, let the kids mate them while they are watching TV.

A drop of household oil will make a zipper slide easier.

---

*The reason why worry kills more people
than work is that more people worry than work.*
—Robert Frost

STAINS

Many stain guides explain how to remove stains using names that take a chemist to pronounce and a pharmacist to find. If I can't remove a stain using products that are in my kitchen or cleaning closet, then I take it to the professionals.

Unwashable Fabrics. I suggest that you don't experiment on unwashable fabrics. If you wanted a piece of clothing enough to pay the high cost of dry-cleaning, then you should also be willing to pay for the services of a professional spotter. Try to get the clothing to the dry cleaners as quickly as possible. Show them the stain and tell them what caused it. If they don't have this information, it is like trying to milk a cow wearing thick gloves and a blindfold—udder confusion.

Some unwashable fabrics can tolerate a very small amount of water. In this case, spots can sometimes be removed quickly just by lightly dabbing the stain with cool water on a slightly damp sponge.

Washable Fabrics. All stains should be treated as promptly as possible before the stain is set. Use ¼ to ½ cup extra laundry detergent when washing stained clothing to give the stain remover an extra boost. **137**

Some stains look as if they have been removed when the fabric is wet, but as it dries the stain will show again. For this reason, wash the stained fabric in hot water and bleach (see Bleaches, page 133).

Avoid using a dryer after stain removal. Many times the stain is invisible while the clothes are still wet, but it shows up again after the drying cycle. Dryer heat may permanently set the stain, so always air-dry stained fabric.

Finally, be patient if the stain doesn't come out on the first try. There are often several different methods for removing a stain (see Stain Removal Guide, page 140). Try them all and repeat them if necessary. Of course, some stains are like freckles: they fade a little with time, but they never go away.

It is easier to keep up than to catch up!

PREWASH STAIN REMOVERS

The first step to eliminating most stains is pretreating the fabric with a good prewash stain remover. There are several pump and aerosol sprays on the market that are well known because of their dazzling commercials and brightly colored bottles, but they are not the only way to escape being mortified by ring-around-the-collar. The following products are very inexpensive to use when compared to the commercial sprays and they are usually just as convenient.

Soap. One of the best prewash stain removers on the market is Fels-Naptha. This is a brown bar of soap. Wet the fabric and the soap, then rub the soap into the stain. Rub the fabric together and rinse. If you cannot find Fels-Naptha in your store, a bar of Lava soap can be used in the same way. One bar of soap will go a long way.

138 **Laundry Detergent.** On many stains you can get good results by pretreating with detergent. Make a paste out of powdered laundry detergent by adding a few drops of water, or use a liquid laundry detergent. Rub it into the stain, rub the fabric together, and rinse.

Prewash Spray. If you like the convenience of a spray, then save yourself the packaging and advertising costs and make your own. Into a pint spray bottle pour ½ cup of ammonia and ½ cup of liquid laundry detergent, such as Era, Dynamo, or Wisk. Fill the rest of the bottle with water, shake it up, and spray it on the stains. Wait at least one minute before putting the stained fabric in the washing machine.

Hairspray. Cheap hairspray that contains lacquer is an excellent prewash spray for many stains. I have removed ink, fruit punch, and lipstick with hairspray when none of the other prewash sprays worked on these stains. It will also eliminate static electricity in permanent press clothes that cling when you are wearing them. Spray it next to your skin, between your slip and dress and/or under the clinging garments.

CLEANING SOLVENTS

For some stains (greasy stains especially), it is necessary to purchase a cleaning solvent. I have had good results with Thoro, Carbona, and Energine (see page 12). Many cleaning solvents are made with naptha or spirits of naphthol, so they are highly flammable. *They should never be used around any heat source* such as a gas dryer, water heater, furnace, or cigarettes. Remove all traces of moisture and fumes before putting fabric treated with a cleaning solvent in the washer or dryer.

Some nonflammable cleaning solvents put out poisonous fumes. Always use cleaning solvents in a well-ventilated area.

Turpentine, Rubbing Alcohol, Fingernail-Polish Remover, Ammonia. These products are used in some stain-removal procedures. Use the same caution as when using a cleaning solvent. Sometimes fabric color or fiber can be damaged by these stain removers, so always test them first in an inconspicuous spot.

THE MYSTERY STAIN

It isn't unusual to be doing the family laundry and suddenly find an unrecognizable blotch. In most cases, it is useless to track down the husband, teenager, or child. They never seem to remember what they were eating or drinking or what they sat in. If you do not know what caused a stain, always take a safe course of action:

1. Rinse the stained area in cold water.

2. Pretreat with a prewash stain remover (see page 138).

3. Rinse (some stains may need to be pretreated and rinsed several times).

4. Wash the fabric using chlorine bleach or all-fabric bleach (see page 133) in the hottest water temperature that is safe for the fabric (page 130). Add extra detergent to the wash water.

5. Air dry.

6. If the stain persists, soak the stain in cold water for thirty minutes.

7. Sponge the stain with a cleaning solvent and let it set for five minutes.

8. Rinse.

9. Repeat steps 2 through 5, if necessary.

STAIN REMOVAL GUIDE

The following is a guide to removal of the most common (and pesky) household stains.

ADHESIVE TAPE. Scrape off the tape with a dull knife. Rub the remaining gummy residue with a white rag dipped in a cleaning solvent.

BLOOD. Soak in cold water for at least thirty minutes or until the stain turns a light brown. Pretreat with a prewash stain remover and rinse. If the stain persists, soak it in a solution of 2 tablespoons ammonia to 1 gallon of warm water.

CANDLE WAX AND PARAFFIN. Solidify the wax by rubbing it with an ice cube, then scrape off as much as possible with a dull knife. Place the fabric beneath a brown paper sack or several layers of white paper towel and press with a warm iron.

CANDY. Soak in warm water with a little detergent added. Pretreat with a prewash stain remover and rinse. If the stain persists, then soak the fabric in 2 tablespoons of chlorine bleach to 1 quart of warm water (test the fabric to make sure it is bleachable—see page 133).

CARBON PAPER. Pretreat with a prewash stain remover and rinse. If the stain persists, put a few drops of ammonia or cleaning solvent on the stain. Rub the fabric together and rinse.

CHOCOLATE OR COCOA. Soak in cold water, then pretreat with a prewash stain remover.

COFFEE AND TEA. Stretch the stained area over a pan or large bowl and secure it with a large elastic band. Pour boiling water over the stain. For delicate fabric, soak in cold water and pretreat with a prewash stain remover. If there was cream in the coffee, the stain may persist. Sponge with a cleaning solvent and rinse.

COSMETICS. Pretreat with a prewash stain remover and rinse. If the stain persists, rub a cleaning solvent in and work with it until all traces of the stain are gone.

CRAYON. Loosen the stain with kitchen shortening and then pretreat with a prewash stain remover. *Plastic dishpan method:* If the stain persists or is widespread (this usually happens when a crayon is washed and dried with the clothes), then use the following method. In a plastic dishpan add ½ cup of powdered dishwashing detergent (or ½ cup of Spic and Span or Soilax) and ½ cup of baking soda. Fill the pan with hot water and put in the clothes. Swish the clothes up and down about every half hour to forty-five minutes for at least eight hours, then wash the stained clothes in the washing machine. Some crayons are made with a permanent dye and nothing will remove them.

DEODORANTS.   Pretreat with a prewash stain remover and rinse.

EGGS.   Scrape off the dried egg and soak the stain in cold water. Pretreat with a prewash stain remover.

FRUIT OR BERRIES.   Treat the same as coffee and tea.

GLUE.   There are many different kinds of glue, and some can never be removed. Check the back of the package for the manufacturer's instructions for cleaning. Fresh glue can be scraped off with a dull knife or washed off with a damp soapy cloth. If the glue is hard then carefully apply drops of hot white vinegar, cleaning solvent *or* fingernail polish remover (without an oil base) over the glue. Put an absorbent cloth over this and then pour more of the removal agent over the cloth. Place a bowl upside-down over the stain to prevent evaporation. Repeat the process every ten minutes until the glue is soft, then scrape it off using the edge of a spoon or butter knife. Wash the area with hot water.

GRASS.   Pretreat with a prewash stain remover (I have found Fels-Naptha will do the best job) and rinse. If the stain persists, sponge with rubbing alcohol (test in an inconspicuous spot first for possible color damage).

GRAVY.   Soak in cold water and pretreat with a prewash stain remover. If stain persists, sponge it with a cleaning solvent.

GREASE AND OIL.   Pretreat with a prewash stain remover, then launder in hot water, using bleach (see page 133). If the stain persists, sponge it with a cleaning solvent.

GUM.   Rub the gum with an ice cube until it becomes hard. Scrap off as much as possible with a dull knife. Dampen a white rag with a cleaning solvent and remove any remaining gum.

INK OR FELT-TIP PEN.   I arrived at work one day just as the doctor's wife was pulling seventeen expensive white shirts out of the dryer. They were beautiful and clean except for the blue splotches on every shirt. She discovered a ball-point pen in the dryer. I had heard that ink could be removed with cheap hair spray containing lacquer. We used a whole can of hair spray on the shirts and then put them back in the washer. They came out of the dryer just as the doctor came home for lunch. There wasn't a blue mark on them.

Rubbing alcohol will also remove ink. Sponge it on and rinse.

LIPSTICK AND ROUGE. Many lipsticks are impossible to remove from fabrics. Pretreat with a prewash stain remover or cheap hair spray and rinse. If the stain doesn't come out, take it to a professional spotter at a dry cleaners.

LIQUOR AND LIQUEUR. Soak in cold water, then pretreat with a prewash stain remover. If it has a fruit base, then treat it as a coffee-and-tea stain.

MAYONNAISE AND SALAD DRESSING. Pretreat with a prewash stain remover. If the stain persists, sponge it with a cleaning solvent.

MILDEW. Sometimes mildew will weaken the fibers of a fabric and the stain is impossible to remove. Pretreat with a prewash stain remover and rinse. Launder in hot water and bleach (see page 133). Take the fabric outside and stretch it out on the grass on a hot, sunny day. Leave it out all day or until the stain is gone.

MILK AND ICE CREAM. Soak in cold water. Pretreat with a prewash stain remover and rinse. If the stain persists, sponge it with cleaning solvent.

MUD. Allow the mud to dry thoroughly and then brush it off. Rinse in cold water and pretreat with a prewash stain remover.

MUSTARD. Rinse off the mustard in cold water. Pretreat with a prewash stain remover and then soak in hot detergent water for several

143

hours. If the stain persists, sponge it with rubbing alcohol. (Test fabric for color-fastness.)

PAINT (OIL BASE). If the stain is allowed to dry, it will be almost impossible to remove, so treat it quickly. Check the label on the can to see what the manufacturer recommends. In many cases, turpentine will remove most of the stain. While the stain is still damp from the turpentine, pretreat it with a prewash stain remover. Soak the fabric in hot water for several hours and then launder.

PAINT (WATER BASE). Soak the fabric in cold water. Pretreat with a prewash stain remover.

PENCIL. Remove the stain with a soft eraser. Pretreat with a prewash stain remover and launder. If the stain persists, apply a few drops of ammonia to it, then pretreat again.

PERFUME. Soak in cold water and pretreat with a prewash stain remover.

PERSPIRATION. Pretreat with a prewash stain remover. (Fels-Naptha works best.) If the stain has discolored the fabric, then sometimes it can be removed by sponging fresh stains with ammonia and old stains with white vinegar. If the stain persists, put the soaking wet garment out in the sun on a hot day.

If perspiration smells cling to a garment, soak it in a solution of 1 gallon water and 1 cup salt.

RING-AROUND-THE-COLLAR. Wet the material with a prewash stain remover. Hold each end of the collar and rub the collar together. Let it set for five minutes before laundering.

SCORCH. If the fabric has been severely scorched, the stain will be impossible to remove because the fibers have been damaged. For less severe scorches, soak the stain in cold water for forty-five minutes, then pretreat with a prewash stain remover. While the fabric is still wet, stretch it out on the lawn on a hot, sunny day. Leave it all day or until the stain is gone.

SHOE POLISH.   Pretreat with a prewash stain remover and rinse. If the stain persists, sponge it with rubbing alcohol. Rinse and launder.

SMOKE.   Pretreat with a prewash stain remover and rinse. If the smoke is greasy, sponge with a cleaning solvent.

SOFT DRINKS.   Some soft-drink stains are invisible when dry, but after heat has been applied or the fabric has aged a few weeks, a yellow stain will appear. Immediately sponge all types and colors (even clear) with cold water. Pretreat with a prewash stain remover and rinse.

TAR (ASPHALT).   This stain may be impossible to remove without damaging the fabric. Act quickly before the stain has time to dry. Scrape off as much of the tar with a dull knife as possible. Pour a cleaning solvent over the stain and sponge until it disappears. Repeat as many times as necessary. Rinse thoroughly. Pretreat with a prewash stain remover and launder.

URINE.   Soak in cold water for thirty minutes. Pretreat with a prewash stain remover and rinse. Urine is highly acidic so it may discolor the fabric. This might be corrected by sponging the stain with ammonia or vinegar. Rinse thoroughly and launder.

VASELINE.   Sponge with a cleaning solvent.

VOMIT.   Rinse off food particles with cold water. To remove the smell, soak the fabric in a solution of 1 cup salt and 1 gallon warm water. Rinse thoroughly and launder.

TIP: To *whiten,* brighten, and remove stains from baby clothes, cottons, polyesters, nylons, badly grayed towels, etc., use the plastic-dishpan method described above under Crayon (page 141).

YOUR NOTES & CLEANING RECIPES

_____

_____

_____

_____

_____

_____

_____

_____

_____

_____

_____

_____

_____

_____

_____

_____

13 Miscellaneous Tips & Recipes

Every housekeeper has a few favorite secrets tucked up her sleeve that don't fall into the categories covered by the earlier chapters in this book. Here are some of mine:

Fireplace. A good method for removing smoke stain out of fireplace stone or brick: Fill a bucket with very hot water and have a nylon brush handy. Cover the hearth with several old bath towels. Pour Coke on the smoke stains and immediately brush it back out with the nylon brush soaked with hot water. Blot the fireplace dry.

Another method is to make a paste of ground pumice stone and ammonia. Spread it over the stain and let it stand for two hours. Rinse with clear water.

Ivory. Stubborn stains on ivory (not piano keys) can be removed by sprinkling salt on the stain, then rubbing it with half a fresh lemon. Rinse and wipe dry.

Brass Knocker. To keep a brass knocker on the front door shining and bright, sprinkle Worcestershire sauce on an SOS pad and scrub. Wipe dry and then rub it with some warmed paraffin wax on a damp cloth. This will preserve its shine and beauty.

Candles and Candleholders. To remove dripped wax from candlesticks, put them in the freezer for a couple of hours or until the wax is frozen and will come off easily. Soak candles in salt water to make them drip-proof.

Pictures. Use a wet fingerprint to mark the spot for the nail when hanging pictures and mirrors.

Painting. When painting, pull a pair of old socks over your shoes to

protect them from splatters and to mop up drips fast with your foot.
Hands. To clean mechanic's grease off your hands, use shaving cream in one hand and sugar in the other. Rub your hands together and wash under hot water.

A homemade hand lotion can be made from:

6 tbs. glycerin
6 tbs. anhydrous lanolin
½ cup petroleum jelly (Vaseline)

Heat these in a double boiler until they melt. Then add

1 tbs. boric acid
several drops of an oil-base perfume

Let this mixture cool, then place it in a pretty bottle for storage. This is great for chapped and dry hands.

Vinegar Tips. The shine on a coat collar and the line left from letting down a hem will disappear if you sponge them with vinegar, then press with an iron on the wrong side of the fabric.

Vinegar will remove fish and onion odors from dishes, utensils, and hands.

More Tips. Wax closet rods for easy sliding of hangers.
Give snow shovels a coat of wax and snow slides right off.
Do not expose pearls to hair spray or perfume. They dull the luster.
Clean jewelry with toothpaste.
To remove broken light bulbs, push a cork into the shreds of glass

and unscrew.

A Personal Tip. When you are working, keep yourself sweet-smelling with this recipe for homemade underarm deodorant.

1 tsp. powdered alum
1 pt. water
A few drops of your favorite perfume

Mix and put it in a spray bottle. This is as effective as commercial deodorant and costs a good deal less.

If you prefer a cream deodorant, mix together equal parts of petroleum jelly, cornstarch, and baking soda and add your favorite perfume. Store in a small jar.

Do it!
Do it right!
Do it right now!

YOUR NOTES & CLEANING RECIPES

INDEX

151

157

About the Authors

Eugenia Chapman and Jill Major are a mother-and-daughter team. Mrs. Chapman has been a professional housekeeper for over forty years. (She loves to clean but hates to write.) Mrs. Major is a free-lance writer. (She loves to write but hates to clean.) They combined their talents to co-author a column called "The Housekeeping Hotline" for the *Deseret News* of Utah. They have also been featured together in hundreds of house-cleaning presentations for TV and radio, including the nationally syndicated TV show, *Hour Magazine*, with host, Gary Collins.

Mrs. Chapman has eleven children—four sons and seven daughters—fifty-six grandchildren and six great grandchildren. (The number of great grandchildren are continually changing and may already have increased by the time of this printing.) She is often asked to give lectures on housekeeping, quick cooking, gardening and family togetherness, for church groups, civic groups and women's clubs. Mrs. Chapman was formerly the head housekeeper in the Lion House, one of the great mansions that Brigham Young built for his many wives.

Mrs. Major is a graduate of the University of Utah. Like her mother, she is a popular speaker, but prefers motivational topics and storytelling. She loves her full-time job of housewife and mother to eight children, but also enjoys pursuing her hobby of writing. Mrs. Major has published articles in local and national newspapers and magazines and has written other books, including a series of children's books.

Helpful Hints from Heloise
America's #1 Lifestyle Manager

___ *All-New Hints from Heloise*

0-399-51510-0/$10.00

A collection of advice for today's busy families from America's most popular household columnist.

___ *Heloise from A to Z*   0-399-51750-2/$10.95

The first household self-help book of Heloise's timeless wisdom for the home to be presented in a convenient, easy-to-use dictionary format.

___ *Heloise Hints for a Healthy Planet*

0-399-51625-5/$7.95

An indispensable guide with hundreds of tips for environmentally sound living both at home and in the workplace.

___ *Heloise Hints for a Single Household*

0-399-51811-8/$8.95

From "the premier household-hints columnist of all time" (*The New Yorker*), an all-new collection of invaluable hints, tips, advice, and inspiration geared towards the special needs of the single household.

___ *Heloise Hints for All Occasions*

0-399-51893-2/$11.00

Heloise shares her strategies for throwing any kind of party anywhere. She provides party planning tips, decorating ideas, and clean-up lessons. Also included is a collection of her classic recipes.